Peer Conflict and Psychological Growth

Marvin W. Berkowitz, *Editor*

NEW DIRECTIONS FOR CHILD DEVELOPMENT
WILLIAM DAMON, *Editor-in-Chief*

Number 29, September 1985

Jossey-Bass Inc., Publishers
San Francisco • London

Marvin W. Berkowitz (Ed.).
Peer Conflict and Psychological Growth.
New Directions for Child Development, no. 29.
San Francisco: Jossey-Bass, 1985.

New Directions for Child Development
William Damon, *Editor-in-Chief*

Copyright © 1985 by Jossey-Bass Inc., Publishers
and
Jossey-Bass Limited

Copyright under International, Pan American, and Universal Copyright Conventions. All rights reserved. No part of this issue may be reproduced in any form—except for brief quotation (not to exceed 500 words) in a review or professional work—without permission in writing from the publishers.

New Directions for Child Development (publication number USPS 494-090) is published quarterly by Jossey-Bass Inc., Publishers. Second-class postage rates are paid at San Francisco, California, and at additional mailing offices.

Correspondence:
Subscriptions, single-issue orders, change of address notices, undelivered copies, and other correspondence should be sent to Subscriptions, Jossey-Bass Inc., Publishers, 433 California Street, San Francisco, California 94104.

Editorial correspondence should be sent to the Editor-in-Chief, William Damon, Department of Psychology, Clark University, Worcester, Massachusetts 01610.

Library of Congress Catalog Card Number 85-60822

International Standard Serial Number ISSN 0195-2269

International Standard Book Number ISBN 87589-796-7

Cover art by WILLI BAUM

Manufactured in the United States of America

Ordering Information

The paperback sourcebooks listed below are published quarterly and can be ordered either by subscription or single-copy.

Subscriptions cost $40.00 per year for institutions, agencies, and libraries. Individuals can subscribe at the special rate of $30.00 per year *if payment is by personal check*. (Note that the full rate of $40.00 applies if payment is by institutional check, even if the subscription is designated for an individual.) Standing orders are accepted.

Single copies are available at $9.95 when payment accompanies order, and *all single-copy orders under $25.00 must include payment.* (California, New Jersey, New York, and Washington, D.C., residents please include appropriate sales tax.) For billed orders, cost per copy is $9.95 plus postage and handling. (Prices subject to change without notice.)

Bulk orders (ten or more copies) of any individual sourcebook are available at the following discounted prices: 10-49 copies, $8.95 each; 50-100 copies, $7.96 each; over 100 copies, *inquire*. Sales tax and postage and handling charges apply as for single copy orders.

To ensure correct and prompt delivery, all orders must give either the *name of an individual* or an *official purchase order number*. Please submit your order as follows:

Subscriptions: specify series and year subscription is to begin.
Single Copies: specify sourcebook code (such as, CD1) and first two words of title.

Mail orders for United States and Possessions, Latin America, Canada, Japan, Australia, and New Zealand to:
 Jossey-Bass Inc., Publishers
 433 California Street
 San Francisco, California 94104

Mail orders for all other parts of the world to:
 Jossey-Bass Limited
 28 Banner Street
 London EC1Y 8QE

New Directions for Child Development Series
William Damon, *Editor-in-Chief*

CD1 *Social Cognition,* William Damon
CD2 *Moral Development,* William Damon
CD3 *Early Symbolization,* Howard Gardner, Dennie Wolf
CD4 *Social Interaction and Communication During Infancy,* Ina C. Uzgiris
CD5 *Intellectual Development Beyond Childhood,* Deanna Kuhn
CD6 *Fact, Fiction, and Fantasy in Childhood,* Ellen Winner, Howard Gardner

CD7   *Clinical-Developmental Psychology,* Robert L. Selman, Regina Yando
CD8   *Anthropological Perspectives on Child Development,* Charles M. Super, Sara Harkness
CD9   *Children's Play,* Kenneth H. Rubin
CD10 *Children's Memory,* Marion Perlmutter
CD11 *Developmental Perspectives on Child Maltreatment,* Ross Rizley, Dante Cicchetti
CD12 *Cognitive Development,* Kurt W. Fischer
CD13 *Viewing Children Through Television,* Hope Kelly, Howard Gardner
CD14 *Childrens' Conceptions of Health, Illness, and Bodily Functions,* Roger Bibace, Mary E. Walsh
CD15 *Children's Conceptions of Spatial Relationships,* Robert Cohen
CD16 *Emotional Development,* Dante Cicchetti, Petra Hesse
CD17 *Developmental Approaches to Giftedness and Creativity,* David Henry Feldman
CD18 *Children's Planning Strategies,* David Forbes, Mark T. Greenberg
CD19 *Children and Divorce,* Lawrence A. Kurdek
CD20 *Child Development and International Development: Research-Policy Interfaces,* Daniel A. Wagner
CD21 *Levels and Transitions in Children's Development,* Kurt W. Fischer
CD22 *Adolescent Development in the Family,* Harold D. Grotevant, Catherine R. Cooper
CD23 *Children's Learning in the "Zone of Proximal Development,"* Barbara Rogoff, James V. Wertsch
CD24 *Children in Families Under Stress,* Anna-Beth Doyle, Dolores Gold, Debbie S. Moscowitz
CD25 *Analyzing Children's Play Dialogues,* Frank Kessel, Artin Göncû
CD26 *Childhood Depression,* Dante Cicchetti, Karen Schneider-Rosen
CD27 *The Development of Reading Skills,* Thomas H. Carr
CD28 *Children and Computers,* Elisa L. Klein

Contents

Editor's Notes 1
Marvin W. Berkowitz

Chapter 1. Conflict Between Children: Social-Cognitive and Sociometric Correlates 3
Carolyn U. Shantz, David W. Shantz
Social understanding in children is related to both the focus and outcome of conflicts during play.

Chapter 2. The Social Origins of Logic: The Contributions of Piaget and Vygotsky 23
Ellice A. Forman, Myra J. Kraker
The capacities for inventing and verifying solutions in problem solving are based in peer interaction.

Chapter 3. Sociocognitive Conflict and Intellectual Growth 41
Nancy Bell, Michèle Grossen, Anne-Nelly Perret-Clermont
Peer conflict about logical problems, under certain specifiable conditions, leads to individual cognitive growth.

Chapter 4. Social Conflict and the Development of Children's Moral and Conventional Concepts 55
Larry Nucci
The nature of peer reactions to social transgressions varies according to the specific social domain of the transgression.

Chapter 5. The Process of Moral Conflict Resolution and Moral Development 71
Marvin W. Berkowitz, John C. Gibbs
The processes whereby peer moral conflict discussion produces moral reasoning development can be understood by direct examination of the peer interactions.

Chapter 6. Peer Conflict in Pair Therapy: Clinical and Developmental Analyses 85
D. Russell Lyman, Robert L. Selman
Strategies for resolving peer conflicts can be understood by studying their development in peer pair therapy.

Index 103

Editor's Notes

Psychologists have long viewed conflict negatively. It has been seen traditionally as indicative of psychological or social breakdown. Peer conflict in children, likewise, has been viewed as, at best, an undesirable disruptive behavior or, at worst, a sign of serious mental disturbance or social retardation. In this volume, we have attempted to present a rather different perspective on peer conflict in children. Our framework is predominantly that of cognitive-developmental psychology. This perspective suggests two broad approaches to the study of peer conflict and psychological growth in children and adolescents.

The first approach suggests that peer conflict itself may be viewed as a developing phenomenon in two different ways. First, forms of peer conflict may lead to the child's development of increased competency in conflict strategies, as the child matures. Chapter Four by Nucci and Chapter Six by Lyman and Selman are prime examples of this point of view. Nucci explores the different peer conflict modes children apply to different developmental domains; he looks specifically at moral versus social-conventional transgressions. Lyman and Selman's research in the context of peer pair therapy demonstrates the development of peer conflict negotiation strategies and its clinical relevance. Second, peer conflict may be mediated by other developing capacities. Chapter One by Shantz and Shantz demonstrates this quite clearly in exploring the social-cognitive correlates of peer conflict modes.

A second broad approach to peer conflict suggested by a developmental orientation focuses on conflict as a potential developmental stimulus. Chapter Three by Bell, Grossen, and Perret-Clermont, Chapter Two by Forman and Kraker, and Chapter Five by Berkowitz and Gibbs are all examples of this perspective. Bell, Grossen, and Perret-Clermont focus on the developmental impetus of early childhood conflicts about logical problems. Forman and Kraker take a more theoretical stance in examining middle adolescent logical problem solving. Berkowitz and Gibbs analyze how peer moral discussions lead to growth in moral-cognitive reasoning in late adolescence. While Bell, Grossen, and Perret-Clermont focus on situational determinants of developmental stimulation, Berkowitz and Gibbs explore the discussion process itself.

These developmental perspectives on peer conflict in childhood and adolescence are relatively new. They have been recognized theoretically for fifty years or more, but it is only recently that they have attracted serious experimental attention. As the contents of this volume demonstrate, the early returns are quite promising.

Marvin W. Berkowitz
Editor

Marvin W. Berkowitz is assistant professor of psychology at Marquette University. His research interests include peer moral discussion and moral development.

What children fight about during play and their degree of success in such fights are related to their understanding of peers and social rules.

Conflict Between Children: Social-Cognitive and Sociometric Correlates

Carolyn U. Shantz
David W. Shantz

In the ongoing interactions of children at play, there are probably no moments as dynamic and problematic as moments of conflict. Whether brief or prolonged, whether they lead to positive or negative outcomes, conflicts between children are those occasions most likely to bring about changes in behavior and thinking of both participants, according to many developmental theories. The three major stage theorists of human development—Piaget, Freud, and Erikson—all posit conflict, either intrapsychic or interpersonal, as a fundamental dynamic in adapatation. There is a central role given to conflict in each theory, although the conceptions of conflict differ from direct opposition to milder "lack of fit" notions: a mismatch between one's conceptions and perceived reality, or incompat-

The research study reported here was supported in part by grant number BNS77-07901 awarded to David W. and Carolyn U. Shantz by the National Science Foundation. Portions of this chapter were reported at the annual meeting of the American Psychological Association, Washington, D.C., 1982. We wish to acknowledge the many contributions to this research by Ellen Cunningham, Diane Jones, Mel Restum, and Thomas Templin.

ibility between the individual's drives and society's rules and demands, or opposing tendencies such as to trust or mistrust others. As such, conflict is one of the broadest, most pervasive, and central concepts in theories of human development.

Despite the theoretical significance of conflict, little research effort has been devoted directly to the topic, particularly to social conflict. Instead, researchers' attention seems to have been captured by behaviors that give rise to and occur within the context of conflict—aggression, anxiety, parental discipline—rather than the state of conflict itself as the context of these behaviors. The direct study of social conflict, albeit modest and sporadic, has occurred in three discernible areas: (a) as a natural social phenomenon between children (for example, Dawe, 1934; Krasnor and Rubin, 1983); (b) as a correlate of social knowledge and reasoning (for example, Spivack and Shure, 1974); and (c) as a process of conceptual change in moral reasoning (for example, Berkowitz and Gibbs, 1983; Damon and Killen, 1982).

The study presented in this chapter is most related to the first two areas of study; it examines the relations between a set of social-cognitive conceptions and various aspects of interpersonal conflict between children. Conflict is defined here as occasions when Child A attempts to influence Child B, Child B resists, and Child A persists. At that point, a state of conflict exists between the two. The mutual resistance in such episodes presents problems and complexities for the participants that are likely, we thought, to maximize the role of social-cognitive factors.

The first questions we examined were whether major aspects of the child's conflict behavior can be predicted (by means of multiple regression analyses) by knowing the developmental level of his or her social-cognitive functioning, and then whether age and gender add to the predictability of conflict behavior. Gender, it bears noting, is seldom studied in such research. Here it is conceptualized as largely a "performance" factor under the assumption that manifested behaviors are the product both of cognitive competencies and socialization. The next question we addressed was whether conflict behaviors relate to children's liking of one another (that is, to their sociometric status).

Unfortunately, very little is known about the major features of conflict between children, or, put otherwise, conflict's "gross anatomy." We selected some aspects that seemed to reflect basic motivational and cognitive features of social interaction: (a) the kinds of issues the child fights about (that is, the child can have the goal to control object use, space use, the other's behavior, physical contact, and/or to change the other's beliefs or ideas); (b) the kinds of behavioral tactics the child uses while fighting (the proportion of his or her total acts that were coded as verbal aggression, physical aggression, commands, or requests); (c) the degree of success the child has (the percentage of conflicts won versus lost or stalemated); and (d) the child's rate of conflict.

We assessed three types of social conceptions rather than a single domain or process, given the evidence that social-cognitive development appears to be quite content- or process-specific (Rubin, 1978; Turiel, 1978). The three selected here were based on an intuitive assessment of relevant conceptions in conflicts: children's understanding of persons, of social rules, and of conflict-resolution strategies. The way children conceive of persons would largely determine, it was thought, how they understand their adversary in an ongoing conflict; that is, it would determine their proclivities to infer internal, psychological events of the peer, such as goals, emotions, attitudes, and so on. Social rule conceptions were assessed because they represent the larger, regulatory social context within which conflict occurs, and rule infractions often lead to conflict (Much and Shweder, 1978). The third type assessed was children's specific knowledge of alternative ways to solve peer conflicts (Spivack and Shure, 1974). The developmental levels of a child's person, rule, and conflict conceptions and their variation indexed social-cognitive functioning.

Conflicts are socially salient and impactful events for the participants and the group and are likely to bear on children's feelings about one another. Thus, the second goal of this study was to relate liking and disliking to various conflict features. To date, most sociometric status research has been restricted to tactics; specifically, physical aggression is related to being disliked (Dodge, 1983).

Four all-boy groups and four all-girl groups were studied in order to duplicate the common same-sex groupings often formed spontaneously in childhood. In each group were equal numbers of six- and seven-year-olds. This age period was chosen because it is a time of substantial change in social-cognitive conceptions and because, in contrast to studies of the preschool ages, conflict has seldom been studied in this age period.

Method

A sample of ninety-six children was randomly selected from among first- and second-grade children who wished to participate and whose parents consented. They came from fourteen different classrooms in two suburban schools that served lower- to upper-middle socioeconomic class, predominately white, neighborhoods. At each school, forty-eight children were randomly assigned to an after-school, free-play group ($N = 12$) with the restrictions that each group have the same gender, equal numbers of first- and second-graders, and no more than three children from the same classroom.

Once a week each of the eight groups met after school in their own school library for one hour of free play for ten consecutive weeks. The play areas (10.5 meters by 10.5 meters) had two tables, four chairs, and two open areas with a wide variety of toys and games. Two graduate students, present at all times to monitor the play and videotape equipment, did not direct or take part in the groups' activities. A complete record of play was made with videotape cameras and microphones.

Behavior Coding. The data base is nine hours of play for each group, the first session being excluded. First, all dyadic conflict episodes were identified on the tapes by teams of observers. Conflict was defined as any sequence in which Child A tried to influence B's behavior, B resisted it, and A persisted. Each conflict episode was coded for the type of outcome (win, loss, stalemate, outside intervention, compromise), and the identity of the winner and loser was recorded. The behaviors that occurred during the course of conflict were coded using an a priori, mutually exclusive set of thirty-eight categories, of which four tactics are focused on here: (a) physical aggression (hitting, slapping, punching, biting, kicking, choking, pinching); (b) verbal aggression (any abusive, insulting, or disapproving remark that was a negative evaluation of the other child, his or her acts, or his or her products); (c) commands (statements ordering or demanding the other child to do something, do it in a certain way, or cease doing something); (d) requests (asking another child to do something or granting permission to the requests to do something).

Each conflict was then coded for the type of issue over which children were fighting, specifically, objects, space, the other's behavior, the other's ideas, or physical contact (touching). Two categories of highest frequency are focused on here: object conflicts, defined as a child's attempt, threat, or act to change, remove, relocate, or destroy an object possessed or claimed by another child, or in any way lay claim to another child's possession; person control conflicts, defined as a child's attempt to make another perform, not perform, or cease a particular act, or to establish, maintain, or avoid social interaction with another child.

Interrater reliability was calculated on eight separate occasions in such a way that raters were unaware which of their coding decisions would be checked. Reliability estimates (number of agreements divided by the sum of all disagreements) averaged 80 percent or higher for all decisions involved in identifying conflict episodes and in coding issues, outcomes, and behaviors.

Social-Cognition Assessments. Each child was interviewed and tested individually on a battery of measures, administered in random order, both prior to and at the end of ten play weeks. The three measures reported here are conceptions of persons, rules, and conflict strategies. All responses were tape-recorded and transcribed verbatim.

Person concepts were elicited by asking the child to nominate a peer whom she or he especially liked and one she or he didn't like very much, and for each "to describe what sort of person she/he is, and what you think of her/him." Each description was divided into informational units and coded for the degree of person descriptiveness, using a modified system by Peevers and Secord (1973). Interrater reliabilities on the fourteen categories for twenty random protocols averaged 93 percent (range: 73 to 100 percent) on both testings. The fourteen categories were combined to form a developmental scale of person concepts, as shown in Figure 1. The levels range from surface aspects of peers that do not differentiate them well as individuals to more psychological descriptions that require inference or abstraction. The level at which most statements occurred defined the child's

Figure 1. Definitions of Developmental Levels of Social-Cognitive Assessments

	Person Conceptions	Rule Conceptions	Conflict Resolution Strategies
Level 1	Person described in terms of possessions, residence, family, or appearance	Failure to rate consistently moral violations as more serious than convention violations; and justifies action as "he/she wanted to do that" or no justification	Forceful strategies: for example, physical attack—grab object, push person; verbal attack; adult intervention
Level 2	Person conceived in terms of social relations often between describer and nominee, as liking, disliking, or friendship	Failure to rate consistently moral violations as more serious than convention violations; and modal reasoning focused on consequences of act for actor or emotional/physical consequences to the victim	Simple conventions and directives: ask, say "please," give command
Level 3	Person described as unique individual with focus on global dispositions, general behavior, roles, and details of acquaintanceship	Consistent rating of moral violations as more serious than convention violations; and modal reasoning focused on consequences of the act for the actor	Reciprocal conventions implying some understanding of reciprocity or meeting needs: taking turns, sharing, trading, offering something for compliance
Level 4	More differentiated and dispositional statements referring to psychological aspects of the person	Consistent rating of moral violations as more serious than convention ones; and modal reasoning focused on consequences to victim, or social standards, or intrinsic principles	Indirect strategies: waiting, ignoring, tricking, finagling, inducing feelings, planning for future

modal developmental level. A second measure of person descriptions, the person variance score, was defined as the number of *different* categories used, ranging from one to fourteen. The variance score here, as well as for the other two tasks, is considered a measure of diversity or flexibility of conceptions.

To assess rule understanding, the raters read five stories of rule violations in random order to each child. Two stories dealt with social-conventional violations—one with not combing one's hair, and another with a boy who preferred to play with dolls—and three stories dealt with moral principle violations—specifically, unprovoked hitting, stealing candy, and not sharing—in order to sample different domains of social rules (Turiel, 1978). After hearing each story, the child rated the seriousness of the rule violation on a five-point scale, ranging from "very good" to "very bad," and explained the reason(s) for the rating. Ten categories of reasons were devised a priori, based on research on story grammars and rule understanding (Damon, 1977; Turiel, 1978). They included general factors of reactions of authorities, peers, or the story character; the physical and emotional consequences to the "victim" or main character; standards and principles of rules; and "no reason." Interrater reliabilities on twenty-six protocols averaged 92 percent (range: 72 to 100 percent).

The developmental level of rule reasoning, formed by combinations of the ten categories, was based largely on Damon's (1977) developmental system. Two criteria define each level: (a) whether or not the child thinks moral rule violations are more serious than violations of social conventions, and (b) the modal type of rationales for the judgment of seriousness. The level definitions, given in Figure 1, give greater weight to the first criteria than to the second in accordance with Damon's view that the first is a critical milestone in children's rule conceptions. The system accounted for 96 percent of the protocols across two testings, providing some initial evidence of its validity (see Shantz, 1982). The variance score was the average number of different rationales given to the five violations (range: one to ten).

The third social-cognitive measure was children's generation of alternative strategies to solve common, hypothetical peer conflicts, adapted from Spivack and Shure (1974). The four social conflict stories, presented in random order, concerned having one's best friend prefer to play with a new peer, wanting to watch a different television show than one's sibling, being bullied on the way to school, and getting a sibling to help in a task. After each story, the child was asked to think of all the different things the story child could do about the problem. Spivack and Shure's (1974) original thirteen categories for preschoolers were used with two additions, "ignore" and "verbal attack." Interrater reliabilities on twenty-five protocols ranged from 80 percent to 100 percent, with an average of 95 percent.

A developmental sequence of four levels was devised by combining the various categories to reflect increasing degree of responsiveness to the psychological aspects of others, increasing subtlety of social influence, and decreasing reliance on immediate gratification and directly taught strategies. An alternative sequence of strategies in developmental levels could be based on value judgments concerning the likely social acceptability or outcomes of such strategies (for example, tricking is less socially acceptable than is sharing). That approach was not adopted here in order to test as directly as possible the degree of strategy sophistication.

Thus, the levels, defined in Figure 1, reflect direct social tactics at one end to more indirect and socially sophisticated ones at the other. The variance score was the number of different strategies (out of the fifteen possible strategies) children generated across stories, and it is the index most frequently used in studies of social problem solving.

Sociometric Measures. Two indices of each child's social status in his or her group, social impact *(SI)* and social preference *(SP)*, were derived from each child's nominations of the three "like most" *(LM)* and three "like least" *(LL)* group members from photographs: $SI = LM + LL$; $SP = LM - LL$ (Peery, 1979). As such, SI is a kind of social visibility indexed by the sum of all nominations, whereas SP is the relative liking of the child by group members. All sociometric and all social-cognitive scores are averages of each child's scores prior to and after the play sessions.

Results

The four aspects of conflict will be considered first in relation to social-cognitive functioning and then in relation to sociometric status.

Conflict Issues. Although children engaged in all of the five kinds of conflicts coded, the average child engaged primarily in object and person disputes (49 percent and 34 percent, respectively, of all of her or his fights). The two issues were highly negatively related ($r = .78$, $p < .001$), indicating that children who had a high percentage of object disputes were involved in a low percentage of person disputes, and vice versa.

To assess the relationship among the social-cognitive scores, age, gender, and the tendency to be involved in person and object conflicts, we performed two multiple regression analyses, entering the social-cognitive scores first, then age, and then gender. With respect to person disputes, the analysis (Table 1) indicates that, taken as a set, a child's social-cognitive scores were significantly related ($mR = .42$, $p < .01$) to the percentage of person fights he or she had, accounting for 18 percent of the variance. This was primarily due to the important role played by the modal person conceptions, which alone accounted for 14 percent of the variance ($mR = .38$, $p < .001$); the addition of the remaining social-cognitive scores did not add significantly to the predictability of person disputes. Further, as the zero-order correlations in Table 2 show, children with higher person conceptions tend to engage in a lower percentage of person fights than do

Table 1. Multiple Regression Analyses: Social Conflict and Social-Cognition, Age, and Sex Predictors ($N = 96$)

	Conflict Variables												
	Issues				Tactics						Outcome		Rate
	Object Control		Person Control		Verbal Aggression		Physical Aggression		Commands		Requests		Wins		Rate of Conflicts
Predictors	mR	R^2	mR	R^2	mR	R^2	mR	R^2	mR	R^2	mR	R^2	mR	R^2	mR	R^2
Social Cognitive																
Person modal	.37[c]	.14[a]	.38[c]	.14[a]	.17	.03	.23[a]	.05[a]	.08	.01	.12	.02	.07	.00	.14	.02
Rules modal	.37[c]	.14	.38[c]	.15	.27[a]	.07[a]	.24	.06	.14	.02	.13	.02	.25[a]	.06[a]	.15	.02
Conflict modal	.39[b]	.14	.40[c]	.16	.27	.07	.24	.06	.15	.02	.13	.02	.26	.07	.15	.02
Person variance	.39[b]	.15	.41[b]	.17	.29	.09	.29	.08	.19	.04	.13	.02	.26	.07	.16	.03
Rules variance	.41[b]	.16	.41[b]	.17	.32	.10	.31	.10	.23	.05	.13	.02	.37[a]	.14[b]	.16	.03
Conflict variance	.41[b]	.17	.42[b]	.18	.32	.10	.31	.10	.27	.07	.19	.04	.37[a]	.14	.20	.04
Age	.41[a]	.17	.42[b]	.18	.35	.12	.33	.11	.27	.07	.27	.07	.38	.14	.27	.07
Gender	.47[b]	.22[a]	.51[c]	.26[b]	.41[a]	.17[a]	.53[c]	.28[b]	.28	.08	.28	.08	.39	.15	.42[a]	.18[a]

[a] $p < .05$ F value of mR and/or increase in R^2
[b] $p < .01$ F value of mR and/or increase in R^2
[c] $p < .001$ F value of mR

Table 2. Correlations Between Conflict Behaviors, Social-Cognition, Age, and Sex ($N = 96$)

	Conflict Variables							
	Issues		Tactics				Outcome	Rate
Social-cognitive measures	Object Control	Person Control	Verbal Aggression	Physical Aggression	Commands	Requests	Wins	Rate of Conflicts
Person modal	.37[b]	-.38[c]	-.17[a]	.23[a]	-.08	.12	.07	.14
Rules modal	.05	.02	-.21[a]	.07	.12	.02	.24[b]	.05
Conflict modal	.00	.10	-.04	.00	.06	.01	.15	-.01
Person variance	-.08	.08	.06	.16[a]	.15	-.03	.08	.07
Rules variance	-.10	.06	.09	.15	.15	.00	-.21[a]	.04
Conflict variance	.04	.04	-.02	.11	.21[a]	.01	-.03	.15
Age	-.02	.03	.08	.18[a]	.07	-.17[a]	.09	.21[a]
Gender	-.27[b]	.34[c]	.24[b]	-.46[c]	-.07	.03	-.13	-.33[c]

[a] $p < .05 = .16$
[b] $p < .01\ .05 = .24$
[c] $p < .001\ .05 = .31$ or greater

those with lower person conceptions, $r = -.38$, $p < .001$. Do age and gender add to the predictability of person conflicts? Age does not; gender does ($r = -.34$, $p < .001$). This indicates that girls tend to become involved in interpersonal control conflicts more than do boys. With all predictors combined—social-cognitive, age, and gender—there is a high relationship to person conflicts ($mR = .51$, $< .001$), or 26 percent of the variance.

Conflicts over the possession and use of objects showed virtually an identical pattern of results with those of person conflicts (see Tables 1 and 2). Again, social-cognitive scores were significantly related to the percentage of object disputes ($mR = .41$, $p < .01$), accounting for 17 percent of the variance, and, again, this is primarily due to the modal person scores (in this case, higher scores were associated with more object disputes). Lastly, age again did not add to predictability, but gender did. The relation between gender and percent object disputes ($r = -.27$, $p < .01$) indicates that boys had a higher percentage of such conflicts than did girls. The analyses of both object and person control conflicts indicate that one's gender predisposes one toward becoming involved in conflicts over particular issues (often objects for boys, and others' behavior for girls) in ways that are not accounted for by differences in social-cognitive functioning.

Tactics Used During Conflict. Children engaged in a wide variety of different behavior during the course of conflicts. The four tactics focused on here accounted for 20 percent of the total acts by the average child in the average conflict: 5 percent physical aggression, 4 percent verbal aggression, 8 percent commands, and 3 percent requests.

Tactics were not as predictable as issues were from the set of six social-cognitive scores, the multiple regression analyses indicated. However, significant zero-order correlations did occur, most often with verbal and physical aggression, not with commands and requests (Tables 1 and 2). With respect to verbal aggression, the set of social-cognitive scores did not bear a significant relation, although two specific measures were so related: Children with more advanced conceptions of persons and rules were less often verbally aggressive than were less advanced children ($r = -.17$ and $-.21$, respectively, both $p < .05$). The age of the child did not add to the predictability, whereas gender did (R^2 increased to .17, $p < .05$). The significant correlation between gender and verbal aggression indicates that girls were relatively higher users of verbal aggression than were boys. All predictors (scores, age, gender) as a set were significantly related to verbal aggression ($mR = .41$, $p < .05$), accounting for 17 percent of the variance.

Physical aggression showed much the same pattern of results as verbal aggression: It was unrelated to social-cognitive scores as a set ($mR = .31$), age did not add to predictability, and gender did, but in an opposite way. There was a strong tendency for boys to aggress physically more often in conflicts than girls ($r = -.46$, $p < .001$). Two specific social-cognitive measures were significantly related: Children with more advanced person conceptions and greater person variance scores showed higher use of physical aggression ($r = .23$ and .16, respectively, both $p < .05$). The entire set of predictors was able to account for a highly significant proportion of variance (28 percent) in physical aggression, with a multiple R of .53 ($p < .001$). It is worth noting that physical and verbal aggression do not appear to be merely different manifestations of a more general aggressive tendency; they are unrelated to one another ($r = .03$) and have somewhat different correlates.

Success in Winning Conflicts. Children's social-cognitive functioning was predictive of their degree of success in winning the conflicts in which they became engaged ($mR = .37$, $p < .05$, accounting for 14 percent of the variance). This relationship was due primarily to two social-cognitive scores: Children who had more advanced rule conceptions won a higher percentage of their disputes than the less advanced, and those who were more consistent in their rule conceptions won more conflicts ($r = .24$ and $-.21$, $p < .01$ and .05, respectively).

It bears noting that three of the four tactics were related to the degree of success (Table 3): relatively high use of commands, and less use of verbal aggression and requests. Success was unrelated to physical aggression ($r = -.05$).

Rate of Fighting. Social-cognitive functioning does not predict the rate at which a child becomes involved in conflicts (that is, the mean number of conflicts per play session) as shown in Table 1. Instead, higher rates of fighting were associated with being a boy, being a second-grader, having few person control fights, and using a higher proportion of physical aggression (in order, $r = -.33, .21, -.18$, and $.67$).

Next, we examine the findings on the relation between conflict behaviors and the child's sociometric status (see Table 3).

Social Impact. The extent to which children were or were not nominated by their group members was highly related ($p < .001$) to two aspects of conflict: the rate of being in conflict ($r = .69$), and the proportionally greater use of physical aggression during conflicts ($r = .54$). In brief, the more contentious and more antagonistic behaviors are strongly related to high social visibility. There is also some tendency for older children, compared to younger, to have higher social impact in these mixed age groups ($r = .23$, $p < .05$).

Social Preference. Relative liking of group members for one another (ranging from highly liked to highly disliked) was related in an opposite way to the same variables, albeit less strongly. Higher likability was associated with engaging in fewer conflicts and less use of physical aggression ($r = -.36$ and $-.16$, respectively, $p < .001$ and .05). Likability was also related to person control conflicts ($r = .16$), but not to age. Neither social preference nor social impact was related to success in winning conflicts.

Table 3. Correlations Among Conflict Variables, Age, Sex, and Sociometric Scores

	Issues		Tactics				Outcome	Rate			Sociometric	
	OC	PC[a]	VA	PA	C	R	W	CPS	Age	Sex[b]	SI	SP
Object control (OC)		-.78[e]	-.44[e]	-.10	-.06	.19[c]	.09	.02	-.02	-.27[d]	-.15	-.07
Person control (PC)			.34[e]	-.21[c]	.08	-.14	.04	-.18[c]	-.03	.34[e]	.03	.16[c]
Aggression:												
Verbal (VA)				.03	-.22[c]	-.18[c]	-.36[e]	.03	.08	.24[d]	.04	-.05
Physical (PA)					-.08	-.24[d]	-.05	.67[e]	.18[c]	-.46[e]	.54[e]	-.16[c]
Commands (C)							.38[e]	.02	.07	-.07	.01	.07
Requests (R)						-.14	-.16[c]	-.14	-.17[c]	.03	.06	.03
Wins (W)								.00	.09	-.13	-.03	.01
Conflicts per session (CPS)									.21[c]	-.33[e]	.69[e]	-.36[e]
Age											.23[c]	-.05
Sex												
Social impact (SI)												-.20[c]
Social preference (SP)												

[a] All variables are percentages of all relevant categories (that is, property is percentage of conflicts over property of the five types of conflicts coded) except conflicts per session, which are frequencies of conflicts.
[b] Negative signs indicate higher percentages (or rates) for boys; positive sign, higher for girls.
[c] $p < .05$–.16
[d] $p < .02$–.24
[e] $p < .001$–.31 or greater

Discussion

The major findings of this study and the focuses of this discussion are (a) children's social-conceptual level of functioning is related most strongly to two aspects of conflict—namely, the issues over which children fight and their success in resolving conflicts; (b) gender, apart from social cognition, adds to the predictability of certain aspects of conflict (specifically, conflict issues, aggressive tactics, and rate); and (c) social visibility and likability within groups are related to the rate of conflict and the use of physically aggressive tactics.

Social Cognition and Conflict Issues. The total set of social-cognitive scores accounted for a significant proportion of variance in the two predominant issues over which children had conflicts—controlling objects and controlling one another's behavior. Zero-order correlations indicated that, within the battery of scores, it was the developmental level of person conceptions that was the primary correlate. Specifically, the higher the children's modal person scores, the less often they were involved in person control conflicts (and the higher those scores, the more they fought about objects). This finding could mean that the more the child conceptualizes peers in psychological, individualized terms, the less the child tries to control his or her peers' behavior, perhaps because their insights into others make them aware of the difficulties of successful control. On the other hand, advanced conceptualizers may attempt control of others frequently, but they are sufficiently skillful that such attempts rarely lead to conflict. This latter possibility cannot be evaluated here because all those situations where influence was attempted and was immediately successful or the attempt was immediately ended are not known; the data of this study include only those situations where influence attempts were resisted and then continued. Further, these two speculations imply a rather direct and causal relation between cognition and behavior, a relation that requires other strategies of study to confirm or disconfirm.

It is possible that the two issues of person control and object control reflect two different, generalized orientations of children. Of the five issues coded, a large percentage fell into object and person codes. This, in itself, could partially account for their negative relationship: The more one fights about one, the less one can fight about the other. However, the magnitude of the relationship suggests that there may well be individual differences in children's tendencies to become involved in disputes over things versus peers' behavior. There is evidence of differences among children in their proclivity to orient toward objects and tasks versus toward people and interpersonal relations, both in preschoolers during free play (Emmerich, 1964; Jennings, 1975) and nine- to twelve-year-olds' self-reports (Nakamura and Finck, 1980).

Over and above the role played by social-cognitive abilities in predicting the issues children get into conflict about, gender played a significant role. Girls' proclivity to engage in person control conflicts and boys' in object control ones are consistent with traditional notions of socialization (for example, Parsons and Bales, 1955)—that is, girls are reared to be relatively more socially oriented and boys more object or task oriented. Given the lack of gender differences in social-cognitive functioning in these children, the results warrant further attention to the independent contribution of gender in predicting issues that give rise to children's disputes. Whether gender differences reflect a more general difference in orientations is not clear at this point. In the three studies just cited on orientation differences, either gender-related differences were not examined or, in one case, they were not found. Suffice it to say that the relation between gender and issues found in this study raises the possibilities that the role of gender is shown either in behaviors for which boys and girls are socialized, or in general orientations toward people or objects, or both.

Social Cognition and Success. Success in achieving one's goals was the second major aspect of conflict highly related to social cognition. This supports the view that social cognition is related to social competency, at least to the extent that social competency is defined as solving social problems in one's favor (Krasnor and Rubin, 1983). This relationship may be particularly evident in conflict situations: Times when one confronts resistance to one's goals would be, presumably, occasions for active, conscious awareness of a social problem and the use of relevant social knowledge and reasoning to reach one's goals. There are many times when children can reach their goals in a rather automated, nonreflective way by direct action or by a peer immediately submitting. Bullies, for example, might have a high success rate by virtue of factors other than advanced social-cognitive abilities. Thus, social-cognitive functioning may be related most clearly to success specifically in conflict situations, not to success in general.

Rule Conceptions and Conflict. Now we turn to the specific social-cognitive predictors of winning conflicts. These predictors consisted of rule conceptions—both their level of development and their consistency in rule reasoning. Why rule conceptions are, apparently, more "potent" than person or conflict strategy conceptions is unclear. It may be specific to the content of the conflict. For example, it could be that a fairly high proportion of property disputes and person control conflicts center on the infraction of rules (for example, taking another's Play-Doh, not abiding by board game rules, interrupting others, using forbidden words, and so on). Children at more advanced levels of rule conceptions may be more sensitive to rule breaking and at an advantage in using the "moral weight" of rule systems to defend their goals. Unfortunately, the coding system used in this study cannot reveal the proportion of issues based on rule violations. It is clear from other data, however, that rules and adherence to them are particularly salient to children of the ages studied here, especially when they concern friendly relations between peers (Selman, 1980; Youniss and Volpe, 1978). A second possibility is that the developmental scale on rule conceptions is the most sensitive indicator of social-cognitive development in general, if such development exists, and the obtained relationship to winning is due to that more than to the specific content of rules. There is partial support for this possibility in that (a) developmental level of rule conceptions was the only developmental scale related significantly to age ($r = .38$, $p < .001$), and (b) it related to one other developmental scale, conflict strategies ($r = .25$, $p < .01$).

Tactics and Social Cognition. The tactics children used to achieve their goals were much less related to social-cognitive functioning than were the goals themselves or the degree of success. Of the twenty-four correlations (four tactics times six social-cognitive scores), only five reached statistical significance. This raises some question about the reliability of the findings. Yet the pattern of correlations is meaningful, particularly because these correlations largely involved the two tactics with the most social impact—verbal and physical aggression. Specifically, children who had more advanced conceptions of rules and persons used less verbal aggression in trying to achieve their goals. Such children may seldom derogate others because they understand the immediately negative emotional consequences for the other child (for example, they may have an empathic response that inhibits name calling), or they view it as counterproductive in changing a peer's behavior (a relationship borne out here: winning and verbal aggression correlated – .36). Another possibility that assumes a less direct relationship between social cognition and verbal aggression is that children with advanced rule and person conceptions are less likely to become involved in person control conflicts, and such conflicts are the ones that tend to elicit verbal aggression. That is, verbal aggression may be related more to the issues at conflict than directly to advanced rule and person conceptions. (Further partial correlations might shed light on this, but they are beyond the scope of this presentation.) The meaning of one other relationship is not clear: Children with advanced person conceptions used proportionally more physical aggression. It probably does not stem from greater involvement in object disputes because such disputes are not related to the tendency to aggress physically. It could be that physical aggression is used sometimes in a rather instrumental and nonhostile way that has less long-term, bad effects on interpersonal relations than does verbal aggression, a personally insulting and derogatory tactic. Finally, it bears noting that there is no evidence for a general "aggressive" tactic: verbal aggression and physical aggression were unrelated (.03), and had many different correlates.

Gender was a significant correlate of tactics. Simply put, girls tended to use verbal aggression and boys, physical aggression. It seems likely that differential socialization, again, in terms of acceptable, expected, and normative behavior for each sex, is reflected here. These tactical differences, it should be recalled, are based entirely on girl-girl and boy-boy interactions; whether greater or lesser differences occur in girl-boy interactions is unknown.

Social Cognition and Rate of Conflict. Do children with advanced social-cognitive skills get into fewer conflicts than less advanced children? One might suppose so if they are better able to avoid conflicts due to their social sensitivities and knowledge; but, one might suppose not if their advanced sensitivities provide more to contest and more "exercising" of their social acumen. The results indicate that neither speculation is tenable: Rate of fighting was unrelated to social-cognitive scores. Instead, the major predictors of rate of conflict were gender and age. Boys tended to get into more conflicts per session than girls, and older children more than younger. To determine whether combination of gender and age (for example, older boys versus younger girls) better predicted conflict rates, follow-up multiple regression analyses were run in which the gender times the age cross-products were entered last. They did not increase predictability of fight rate)or any other aspect of conflict. These results confirm the general picture from studies of aggression: Boys are more likely, on the whole, than girls to engage in higher rates of fighting and use more physical aggression in trying to resolve disputes.

Peer Status and Conflict. Children's perceptions and feelings about one another, as indexed by their nominations of "most liked" and "most disliked" peers in their group, revealed some equally interesting relations to various aspects of conflict. Children who were involved frequently in conflicts had high social impact in their groups and were relatively more disliked. And, since there is a high relationship between rate and physical aggression, it is not surprising to find that physical aggression is also related to high impact and low preference. Whereas sociometric research has documented that being disliked or having rejected status is closely related to being physically aggressive with peers (Dodge, 1983, for example), the data of this study extend this picture of peer relations. It is frequent contentious behavior (with and without physically aggressive tactics) that is especially related to high visibility and low likability.

General Conclusions. There are some larger aspects of the findings of this study that merit discussion. First, social-cognitive functioning was more highly related to issues than to specific tactics. Issues may be conceptualized as goals of the contesters: to control an object or to control another's behavior. Further, there may be many simultaneous, even hierarchically arranged, goals in any one conflict episode. Besides control over things or events, one presumably has goals to have a favorable outcome for the self, to maintain or create good relationships with one's adversary, and so on. To the extent the issues of conflict as coded here are viewed as contestors' goals, this study joins a recent and diverse group of studies that have documented the importance of children's goals in revealing cognition/behavior relations. The premise, briefly put by Renshaw and Asher (1983), is that "situations themselves do not define the goals for children. Instead, children must formulate, however tentatively or even unconsciously, social goals to pursue in particular situations" (p. 355). In conflict situations, both hypothetical and real, researchers have found that older children (Renshaw and Asher, 1983) and girls (Forbes and others, 1984) have goals to maintain good relationships with their adversaries whereas younger children and boys have individualistic or object-oriented goals. Further, Krasnor and Rubin (1983) found that preschoolers' success in solving social problems (to get a toy, get attention, begin a conversation, and so on) was more predictable by knowing the specific goal of the child than by knowing the specific strategy used. Because different behaviors can serve to achieve the same goal and similar behaviors can be means to reach different goals, there may have been a premature "rush to judgment" in the field that tactics or strategies—or all the different aspects of conflict— would be most closely related to social-cognitive development. But is is not a matter of future research focusing on either goals or tactics, but rather it should focus on tactics *in relation to* different goals; that is, the likelihood of using particular tactics and the success of specific tactics are likely to vary with the types of goals. For example, the goal of controlling another's behavior in common social situations would seem, in general, to "pull for" more verbal than physical tactics compared to the goal of controlling an object. Although in the present study the correlations of only one tactic—verbal aggression—give some support to this proposition, Krasnor and Rubin (1983) found clearer evidence that strategies varied with the goal in their effectiveness.

Gender differences were widespread, appearing as significant predictors in virtually all aspects of conflict studied here. They are notable because they are seldom studied in reserach in social-cognition/behavior relations, but they deserve to be in future research. Perhaps because the source of most social-cognitive research on children stems from Piaget's theory of mental development, which is indifferent to individual differences, and because, empirically, few gender differences have been found in social-cognitive tasks (see Shantz, 1983, for a review), researchers have tended to neglect gender differences when they have moved into social behavior in relation to social-cognitive functioning (or they studied one gender only). But to reveal how social-cognitive competencies are manifested in social behavior, gender differences may well have to be taken into account. At the same time, we should note that not all studies of natural conflicts have found gender differences in goals and tactics (for example, Krasnor and Rubin, 1983).

Finally, the way social-cognitive functioning was assessed in this study is exploratory, particularly the construction of developmental scales to reveal central tendencies (modal level) of conception and variance. The scales, while related to other research (for example, Peevers and Secord, 1973; Selman and Demorest, 1984), require independent evidence of reliability and validity. At this point, the results hint at the greater import of modal level than variance in relating cognition to behavior and further hint at broader "domains" (content) rather than highly specific domains. In the latter case, one might have expected that children's reasoning about conflict specifically, compared to conceptions about people in general and social rules in general, would relate most highly to conflict behaviors of various kinds. Such an expectation would follow the dictum "the more specific the content of reasoning is to the behavior to be predicted, the closer the relationship to be found." In this study, there was a notable absence of correlations between conflict strategies generated to hypothetical peer conflicts (whether measured by developmental level or by the number of different strategies) and virtually any aspect of conflict behavior. Such findings suggest that extensive theoretical and empirical work lies ahead to determine which domains (of innumerable relevant domains) and which degree of specificity of domains are needed to reveal the elusive relations between social behavior and social-cognitive development.

References

Berkowitz, M. W., and Gibbs, J. C. "Measuring the Developmental Features of Moral Discussion." *Merrill-Palmer Quarterly,* 1983, *29,* 399-410.
Damon, W. *The Social World of the Child.* San Francisco: Jossey-Bass, 1977.
Damon, W., and Killen, M. "Peer Interaction and the Process of Change in Children's Moral Reasoning." *Merrill-Palmer Quarterly,* 1982, *28,* 347-367.
Dawe, H. C. "An Analysis of 200 Quarrels of Preschool Children." *Child Development,* 1934, *5,* 139-157.
Dodge, K. A. "Behavioral Antecedents of Peer Social Status." *Child Development,* 1983, *54,* 1386-1399.
Emmerich, W. "Continuity and Stability in Early Social Development." *Child Development,* 1964, *35,* 311-332.
Forbes, D., Danaher, D., and Miller, P. M. "Sex Differences in Children's Social Development: Gender-Related Strategies for Coping with Interpersonal Conflict." Unpublished paper, Harvard University, 1984.
Jennings, K. D. "People Versus Object Orientation, Social Behavior, and Intellectual Abilities in Preschool Children." *Developmental Psychology,* 1975, *11,* 511-519.
Krasnor, L. R., and Rubin, K. H. "Preschool Social Problem Solving: Attempts and Outcomes in Naturalistic Interaction." *Child Development,* 1983, *54,* 1545-1558.
Much, N. C., and Shweder, R. A. "Speaking of Rules: The Analysis of Culture in Breach." In W. Damon (Ed.), *Moral Development.* New Directions for Child Development, no. 2. San Francisco: Jossey-Bass, 1978.
Nakamura, C. Y., and Finck, D. N. "Relative Effectiveness of Socially Oriented and Task-Oriented Children and Predictability of Their Behaviors." *Monographs of the Society for Research in Child Development,* 1980, *45* (3-4).
Parsons, T., and Bales, R. F. (Eds.). *Family, Socialization, and Interaction Process.* New York: Free Press, 1955.

Peery, J. C. "Popular, Amiable, Isolated, Rejected: A Reconceptualization of Sociometric Status in Preschool Children." *Child Development,* 1979, *50,* 1231-1234.

Peevers, B. H., and Secord, P. F. "Developmental Changes in Attribution of Descriptive Concepts to Persons." *Journal of Personality and Social Psychology,* 1973, *27,* 120-128.

Renshaw, P. D., and Asher, S. T. "Children's Goals and Strategies for Social Interaction." *Merrill-Palmer Quarterly,* 1983, *29,* 353-374.

Rubin, K. H. "Role Taking in Childhood: Some Methodological Considerations." *Child Development,* 1978, *49,* 428-433.

Selman, R. L. *The Growth of Interpersonal Understanding.* New York: Academic Press, 1980.

Selman, R. L., and Demorest, A. P. "Observing Troubled Children's Interpersonal Negotiation Strategies: Implications of and for a Developmental Model." *Child Development,* 1984, *55,* 288-304.

Shantz, C. U. "Children's Understanding of Social Rules and the Social Context." In F. C. Serafica (Ed.), *Social-Cognitive Development in Context.* New York: Guilford, 1982.

Shantz, C. U. "Social Cognition." In J. H. Flavell and E. Markman (Eds.), *Handbook of Child Psychology.* Volume 3: *Cognitive Development.* (4th ed.) New York: Wiley, 1983.

Spivack, G., and Shure, M. B. *Social Adjustment of Young Children.* San Francisco: Jossey-Bass, 1974.

Turiel, E. "Social Regulations and Domains of Social Concepts." In W. Damon (Ed.), *Social Cognition.* New Directions for Child Development, No. 1. San Francisco, Jossey-Bass, 1978.

Youniss, J., and Volpe, J. "A Relational Analysis of Children's Friendships." In W. Damon (Ed.), *Social Cognition.* New Directions for Child Development, no. 1. San Francisco: Jossey-Bass, 1978.

Carolyn U. Shantz received her degree in clinical psychology at Purdue University in 1966. Her research interests are in social-cognitive and cognitive development. She is professor of psychology at Wayne State University, Detroit, Michigan.

David W. Shantz received his degree in clinical psychology at Purdue University in 1966. His research has focused on aggressive behavior of children and its social and social-cognitive correlates. He is chair of the Department of Psychology, Oakland University, Rochester, Michigan.

The theories of Piaget and Vygotsky suggest that peer interaction can play an important role in two aspects of problem solving: inventing solutions and verifying them.

The Social Origins of Logic: The Contributions of Piaget and Vygotsky

Ellice A. Forman
Myra J. Kraker

In the late nineteenth and early twentieth centuries, a number of major psychological theorists (for example, G. H. Mead, J. M. Baldwin, J. Piaget, and L. S. Vygotsky) speculated about the social origins of thought. "We must regard mind . . . as arising and developing within the social process, within the empirical matrix of social interactions" (Mead, 1934, p. 133). However, empirical support for these ideas is just now being reported in the literature. The bulk of the current research relies upon Piaget's early writings (1926, 1928, 1950, 1965) concerning the influence of peer inter-

An earlier version of this chapter was presented by Ellice Forman at the Twelfth Annual Symposium of the Jean Piaget Society, Philadelphia, June 1982. This research was supported, in part, by NIMH grant number 5T32MH15786 to the Department of Psychology, Northwestern University. The authors gratefully acknowledge the cooperation and support of Richard Lesh and the administration, faculty, parents, and students of the M. L. King, Jr., Experimental Laboratory School, Evanston, Illinois. We would also like to thank Addison Stone for his invaluable assistance in all phases of the research, and Caroline Anderson, Marsha Landau, Leonard Scinto, and Sue Sugarman for their comments on earlier drafts of this chapter.

action on children's cognitive development. In this work, Piaget identified two main functions of intelligence: inventing solutions and verifying them (1928). It was the second function, logical verification, that he claimed arises as a response to real or anticipated social opposition.

Piaget's early interest in the social nature of adult thought stemmed from his desire to explain some of the peculiar properties of child thought. According to Piaget, a primary characteristic of the thought of preschool children is their tendency to center on one particular state of an object or on one point of view of reality. For example, young children seem unable to coordinate past and present appearances of an object array, a conceptual skill necessary for conservation of length, volume, or mass. Also, they do not seem to recognize that multiple perspectives on an object array must be integrated in order to arrive at a complete, objective conception of the array. Piaget felt that peer interaction can help children decenter their thinking because this social context can provide both conflict between opposing centrations and social incentives to coordinate them.

Several concepts are central to Piaget's view of social experience. First, his interest in peer interaction is in its ability to foster cognitive conflict. Conflict for Piaget is crucial because it creates disequilibrium or a mismatch between one's internal cognitive structures and the environment. When disequilibrium occurs, it produces internal structural changes or accommodations in order to assimilate the new information. Disequilibrium and the resulting internal adjustments are, for Piaget, the primary causes of cognitive development. Thus, peer interaction derives its importance from its ability to affect equilibration.

Second, Piaget stressed peer interaction rather than adult-child interaction. Although young children have to adjust their behavior in order to comply with adult demands, Piaget felt that this behavioral compliance does not require any internal cognitive adjustments. In contrast, children are more likely to challenge the demands of peers and to attempt to reconcile any differences between their own ideas and those of others. It is this process of peer conflict and coordination that can result in the disequilibrium necessary for development.

Finally, Piaget felt that social coordination can result in cognitive development if the consensus that emerges is achieved through a process of active cognitive restructuring in the participants. Consensus achieved by other means (submission to authority or passive acceptance) is not seen as producing the disequilibrium necessary for development.

Therefore, Piaget felt that peer interaction influences logical verification in the following way: When speakers attempt to present their ideas to an audience of peers, they often discover that their audience does not agree with them. In order to convince others of the validity of their position, they need to develop a convincing argument—one that is logically sound and is based on supportive evidence. The audience, in turn, may develop their own arguments, which could depend on evidence that disconfirms the original speaker's position. If genuine consensus is to be achieved, the entire group must be able to agree upon a position that integrates evidence from all the original positions. Thus, logical verification, as it occurs in a peer interactional context, should exhibit social as well as cognitive conflict between opposing perspectives on a problem. In addition, the resolution of conflict should be achieved through an active process of negotiation.

Piaget's provocative theorizing about the social origins of thought for the most part was not pursued in his later research endeavors. Because Piaget spent the rest of his life articulating a theory of cognitive development in which social factors played a quite minor role, investigators are just now beginning to explore the implications of his early speculations. In particular, his speculations seem to have their greatest application in the area of logical verification—that is, in the child's growing ability to present logical arguments to others, to acknowledge opposing arguments, to incorporate several positions, and to reach a consensus. Although in Piaget's later work on equilibration he became more interested in the topic of logical invention, he never articulated a role for peer interaction in this aspect of thought.

The complementary interests of another major developmental theorist, L. S. Vygotsky (1962, 1978), may shed light on the social origins of invention. Vygotsky was interested in describing emerging cognitive skills within instructional contexts. He felt very strongly that in order to understand any kind of skill, one needs to study it genetically. He argued that one way to accomplish this aim would be to study children's performance in instructional contexts over short periods of time. The emergence of new problem-solving skills could be charted in these contexts as varying amounts of social assistance were provided by the instructor.

After examining adult-child interaction using this procedure of microgenetic analysis (Wertsch and Stone, 1978), Vygotsky concluded that social interaction with adults or more capable peers can enable children to solve new problems with assistance before they can solve them alone. Vygotsky called this difference between what a child can do alone and what he or she can be led to do with assistance the zone of proximal development. He observed that, over time, the transfer of problem-solving control goes from the adult to the child—from interpsychological regulation to intrapsychological regulation. How is this achieved? One of the clearest examples of this process has been described in a study of adult-child problem solving by Wertsch (1979).

Two ideas are important in Wertsch's microgenetic analysis. First, when the two participants (for example, a mother and her preschool child) begin to work on a problem, their individual conceptions of the task goals and procedures are quite different. Over time, they develop an increasingly similar definition of the task situation as the adult observes, guides, and corrects the child who carries out as many of the task procedures as possible. The definition of the task situation is rarely or never made explicit but is jointly constructed as other-regulation becomes self-regulation. When the child has finally mastered the task, the child and the adult share a common definition of the task situation.

Second, what the adult provides for the child is strategic or metacognitive information about the task. That is, the child is thought to have the component skills necessary to do the task, but it is assumed that he or she does not know how to assemble those skills in the correct order, how to interpret the task goal, or how to monitor his or her behavior. These strategic skills are provided by the adult and are gradually internalized by the child.

One can use Vygotsky's theory to hypothesize that, in certain circumstances, peers may be able to provide the same kind of support and guidance for each other that adults provide. For example, when two peers are presented with a new problem to solve in a collaborative fashion, neither of them may have a solution in mind. In fact, they may not even know how to begin: what the goal of the problem might be, what subtasks the problem might contain, what resources they might need. One strategy that peers sometimes use in this situation is to have one person try a familiar problem-attack approach, such as summarizing the available data. As he or she does this, the partner watches, evaluates, and proposes alternative strategies. The collaborators' immediate goal seems to be pragmatic: to figure out the best way to solve and understand that particular problem. Their actions are directed at co-constructing an implicit understanding of the task and a set of procedures for solving it. The interaction may be largely or entirely nonverbal and may display little or no social conflict. Unlike logical verification, invention does not require that one can explain one's activities. The common understanding that collaborators co-construct is largely implicit.

In summary, both of the two functions of intelligence identified by Piaget, inventing solutions and verifying them, may be facilitated by the social environment. In Piaget's early work, he hypothesized a role for peer interaction in the process of logical verification. Vygotsky's research on emerging cognitive skills can be used to argue that peer interaction may also provide a fertile environment for logical invention.

Previous Research on the Social Origins of Logic

The bulk of the recent empirical work on the social origins of logical thought has been guided by Piaget's ideas. The largest body of research of a programmatic nature has been done by Willem Doise and his colleagues in Geneva (Doise and Mackie, 1981; Doise and others, 1975, 1976; Mugny and others, 1981; Perret-Clermont, 1980; Bell and others, Chapter Three of this volume). The Genevan research group has begun to generate support for some of Piaget's ideas and to qualify some of his other hypotheses. They have demonstrated that progress in concrete operational reasoning can be made by exposing children to certain kinds of peer interactional contexts. Some contexts seem to stimulate greater gains in reasoning than do others. The contexts most likely to induce change are those high in cognitive conflict, social conflict, or both. Conflict can be induced in a variety of ways—for example, by pairing subjects whose pretest scores are moderately discrepant or by exposing subjects to one or more incorrect and conflicting perspectives. Exposure to cognitive conflict may not be sufficient for inducing cognitive restructuring in subjects younger than nine years if verbal interaction is not permitted or if the social structure encourages passive compliance.

To a large degree, the Genevan research has remained well within Piaget's model of the role of social factors in development. The researchers' primary interest in peer interaction has been in its ability to generate conflict or disequilibrium, which can lead, in turn, to cognitive restructuring and growth. This view of socially induced cognitive growth is consistent with Piaget's early hypothesis that social factors operate in logical verification. In order for a cognitive conflict to occur, the children must differ in their conceptions of the problem solution. For a truly coordinated solution to emerge, arguments supporting and refuting their initial positions must have been proposed by the participants, and a process of active cognitive restructuring must have occurred.

Unfortunately, the Genevan research and similar work by other investigators (Bearison, 1982; Emler and Valiant, 1982; Glachan and Light, 1982) have utilized an experimental paradigm, the training study, that does not allow one to examine either social or cognitive processes directly. Instead, subjects are individually pretested and assigned to different treatment groups in which the degree of conflict is experimentally manipulated. Then the effects of these treatments on cognition are assessed by computing each child's pretest-to-posttest gain score. When differences in cognitive gains among the treatment groups are found, the differences are attributed either to social conflict, cognitive conflict, or both.

The training study paradigm has some serious limitations, despite its ability to demonstrate that peer interaction is capable of inducing cognitive growth under experimental conditions. First, the "hard" data from such research lie in the individual pretest and posttest scores. Data about the social and cognitive processes that might have occurred during the treatment are rarely gathered in a systematic fashion and are reported anecdotally, if at all. Second, average group gains in the outcome measures are reported, not individual scores. Thus, the fact that some peer interactions may be more facilitative of cognitive restructuring than others is obscured. Third, the training study paradigm can only demonstrate the effect of different social experiences on cognitive achievements (for example, a change from an incorrect to a correcct judgment on a conservation task) not on cognitive processes (for example, the ability to utilize disconfirming evidence). Fourth, it provides no information about how peer interaction may influence the development of reasoning and problem solving in more naturalistic contexts over time. In effect, data that can tell us *how* peer interaction can affect either logical invention or logical verification are not being collected or analyzed in this research.

Many investigators are now recognizing the need to observe the social and cognitive coordination processes as they occur during problem solving (Bearison, 1982; Perret-Clermont, 1980), but only a few have attempted to do so in a systematic fashion (Forman and Cazden, in press). However, a change in methodology from an experimental paradigm to an observational one has several important procedural and theoretical implications.

First, observational methods traditionally have been used in social developmental research by investigators with goals and theoretical orientations which are quite different from those of cognitive developmentalists. Kuhn (1978) and Forman (1983) have argued that the majority of the cognitive developmental research shares an organismic or contextualistic theoretical model (Overton and Reese, 1973; Pepper, 1942), while the bulk of the social developmental research uses a mechanistic model. That does not mean that naturalistic observations cannot be used to study cognitive processes. What it does imply, however, is that the typical procedures used to collect, code, and analyze observational data may have to be modified in order to address both cognitive and social questions from a consistent theoretical perspective.

Second, an observational methodology precludes the kind of exhaustive probing of an individual subject's reasoning that the Piagetian clinical method or American modifications of that method require. Thus, one is forced to base one's inferences about cognition upon observable behavior that is often inconclusive and ambiguous.

Third, when observing two or more people attempting to solve a problem in a collaborative fashion, one frequently sees concepts and strategies emerge through a process of co-construction. Often, one is viewing cognition as it is enacted on the social plane—as an activity that two or more people share. This perspective on cognition was articulated by one subject in a study of collaborative problem solving (Forman and Cazden, in press). The nine-year-old boy turned to his partner and said, "You be the memory man." By saying this, he was explicitly labeling their ongoing joint cognitive activity in which his role was to select new chemical combinations to test and his partner's job was to remember their previous tests in order to avoid duplications. This view of shared cognitive activity contradicts the notion of cognition as something that operates exclusively within people's heads.

Finally, if one assesses both shared and individual cognitive activity in one study (by observing the problem-solving activity and by administering pretests and posttests), one may find an inconsistency between the two. For example, Forman (Forman, 1981; Forman and Cazden, in press) found that some collaborative partners demonstrated a higher level of combinatorial reasoning in a social context than they did individually. Thus, socially achieved cognitive activities may be internalized incompletely by the participants. This position is consistent with that of Vygotsky, who proposed that new cognitive functions would appear first on the social plane and then be internalized. A similar position has begun to appear in the recent writings of the Genevan group as well (Doise and Mackie, 1981; Mugny and others, 1981).

An Exploratory Study of Peer Collaboration

As an example of how joint cognitive activity can be observed, we will present some data from an ongoing exploratory study of collaborative problem solving in adolescents. The purpose of the following presentation is twofold: to describe the kind of task environment in which change over time in cognitive processes can be observed and to illustrate the processes of logical invention and verification in the context of peer collaboration.

The task used in this study involved the projection of shadows of geometric shapes onto a screen. Six geometric shapes (a circle, an equilateral triangle, a right angle, a right triangle, a square, and parallel lines) were presented, one at a time, to the subjects. For each geometric shape, the subjects were asked to sequence their activities in the following way:

1. *Prediction Decision Phase.* With the light off, the subjects predicted which of six line drawings of shadows could be projected from a given geometric shape that was mounted on a stand. For example, the line drawings that were presented with the circle were a small circle, a large circle, an ellipse, an egg, a straight line, and a half circle.

2. *Prediction Justification Phase.* The examiner asked the subjects to explain their predictions for each of the six shadow line drawings.

3. *Testing Phase.* The subjects turned on the light, tested their predictions, and traced the shadows on a pad that served as the screen.

4. *Evaluation Phase.* The light was turned off and the examiner asked for explanations of the results of the testing.

Thus, the shadows task was structured as a sequence of recurring phases of activity. These phases allow one to observe how subjects investigate a problem under differing amounts of examiner guidance. In addition, they permit the observation of subjects' repeated attempts to predict, test, or evaluate across the six geometric shapes. This structure enables us to segment the stream of behavior into episodes defined by subjects' activity. Also, recurrent activity episodes within and between shapes allow us to document change over time.

For example, one can compare subjects' predictions about the shadows that can be made by a particular shape with the subjects' testing of that shape. One can also compare the explanations partners give each other for their predictions and conclusions during the first and third phases with those they give the examiner during the second and fourth phases. Finally, one can assess whether subjects' reasoning and problem-attack skills change over time: Is their reasoning about the first triangle less general and articulate than their reasoning about the second triangle? The result of this task structuring is that comparisons do not need to be made between contiguous events or between specified types of behavioral acts but can easily be made between related, goal-directed activities. (See Kuhn and Phelps, 1982; Stone and others, 1983; and Wertsch and others, 1980, for examples of how a similar kind of task structuring can be used to observe cognitive strategies in other social and task environments.)

The twelve subjects of this study (eight girls and four boys) were selected from one seventh-grade classroom in a suburban Chicago school. The subjects were assigned to one of two problem-solving conditions (dyadic or individual). Each of the four dyads was matched to an individual based on their performance on two pretests, the Monash Space Visualization Test (Clements and Wattanawaha, 1978) and a test of formal operations developed by Tisher (1971). The dyads were composed of subjects with approximately similar pretest performance levels.

The videotapes of the problem-solving sessions will enable us to compare the dyads and individuals on a number of dimensions of cognitive and social strategy usage. Analyses of problem-solving activity are presently being conducted. Complete results from these analyses are not yet available. However, the results of two preliminary comparisons indicate that the dyads and individuals do differ on some global indices. First, the dyads spent more time, on the average, in the testing phase of the task than did the individuals (thirty-six minutes, forty-five seconds, and twenty-six minutes, thirty-six seconds, respectively). Both groups spent equivalent amounts of time on the prediction decision phase. Second, the dyads were more likely to revise their predictions after testing them than were the individuals (13.5 revisions for the dyads versus 8.25 revisions for the individuals).

Why did the dyads spend more time testing their hypotheses than did the individuals? Why were they more likely to revise their hypotheses in response to disconfirming feedback? Although we do not yet have the data to answer these questions, we can use an example to illustrate what some dyads did when they made predictions and tested them in this task.

We have selected several segments from a transcript of the first problem-solving session of the dyad composed of Karen and Steven. The segments selected for presentation were those in which the subjects attempted to determine whether or not an egg-shaped and an elliptical shadow could be projected from a circle.

The transcript segment begins with the prediction justification phase of the circle task. The examiner asked the subjects, collectively, about each of the six line drawings. In order to avoid supplying the subjects with convenient geometric labels for the drawings, they were labeled Figures 1 through 6. The egg-shaped drawing was Figure 4, the elliptical drawing (displayed in a vertical position) was Figure 6. Previously, the subjects had decided, between themselves, that neither an elliptical nor an egg-shaped shadow could be made.

(1) E(Examiner): OK, and why don't you think you can make Figure 4?
(2) K(Karen): Impossible, I think, I don't know.
(3) S(Steven): Wait a minute, it's . . . *(K picks up the line drawing of the egg shape)*. . . just a minute, if you were to go like this . . . *(S tilts the circle on the stand.)*
(4) K: I don't know *(K hands line drawing of egg to S.)* It seems a little odd.
(5) S: I think, it might be possible, but I don't think it's probable, but if you were to tilt it like this . . . *(S tilts line drawing toward and away from light.)* If this *(S gestures with the line drawing)* was this . . . *(S touches the circle)* you were to tilt it like this, it might . . . S tilts circle.)*

. . .

(6) E: *Ah, what about Figure 6?*
(7) S: Six, where is it? This one? *(S studies the drawing of the ellipse briefly.)*
(8) E: Yeah.
(9) S: What do you think? *S gives the drawing to K. K glances at the geometric circular shape on the stand and examines the drawing carefully.)*
(10) K: Uh . . . Hmm . . . not really.
(11) S: Yeah.

During the prediction decision phase of the task, Karen and Steven had decided that neither of these two figures could be made, but, when asked to explain their predictions to the examiner, their answers revealed some subtle differences in thinking between the two. Karen is dubious about both figures. At first, she volunteers her opinion that it would be impossible to make an egg-shaped shadow but immediately qualifies that answer (line 2). When Steven indirectly asks her to reconsider her answer by proposing that tilting the top half of the circle toward the line might produce such a shadow (line 3), she reaffirms her doubts about the shape (line 4). To Steven, the egg-shaped shadow seems possible but not certain. He seems even less certain about the ellipse and seeks Karen's opinion (line 9) before venturing his own (line 11). As you can see, neither subject has a firm hypothesis about either of these two shapes. Sometimes they seek confirmation from the other, and sometimes they propose a slightly different position. However, their ideas are quite tentative at this point. In the next segment of transcript, they are testing their predictions with the light on.

(12) K: I think if you put it back *(K moves the stand toward the light)*, it looks more like the oval *(egg shape)*. *(S holds the line drawing of the egg next to the shadow on the screen.)*

(13) S: I don't think so. *(K pulls the stand toward the light and rotates the circle. S helps her.)*

(14) K: Uh-huh. It's got straight lines. *(K notices that as you rotate the circle 90°, you get a shadow of a straight line.)*

(15) S: Yeah, the straight lines work except for these things *(clamps on the stand)* we gotta ignore. *S rotates the circle and an ellipse appears in a horizontal position.)*

(16) K: Wait a sec. *(K points to the elliptical line drawing.)*

(17) S: *(S ignores K's pointing.)* Doesn't this bend down? *(S attempts to bend the geometric shape in a direction not permitted by the stand.)* No, it doesn't.

At first, Karen seems more willing than Steven to see if they can produce an egg-shaped shadow (lines 12 and 13). She tries moving the stand on which the circle is attached toward and away from the light and rotating the circle on the stand. Notice here that it is Karen who moves the shape in order to produce an egg-shaped shadow and Steven who assumes the role of observer and critic (lines 12 and 13). The roles have reversed from the previous segment of transcript and will reverse again.

As a consequence of rotating the circle, Karen observes two shadows: a horizontal straight line and a horizontal ellipse (lines 14 and 16). She explicitly labels the straight line, which matches one of the other six line drawings they are testing. She does not label the ellipse but indicates her recognition of it by pointing to the elliptical line drawing. Steven, however, only notices the straight line (line 15). The testing continues in the next segment.

(18) K: What about this one? *(K considers the egg-shaped line drawing again.)*

(19) S: Hm-m gosh. I don't know. *(S attempts to match the drawing to the shadow.)*

(20) K: No.

(21) S: No, wait a minute. *(S holds the egg line drawing against the screen.)* See how it's almost getting there? *(S gradually turns the shape. K observes S adjust the shadow.)* It doesn't go in anymore. Yeah, this one works. *(K pulls the stand back.)*

(22) K: Move it a little bit. *(S holds the drawing against the screen.)*
(23) S: *(S adjusts the position of the stand.)* So, just a little bit. This has got to go down more.
(24) K: No.
(25) S: I think that'll be all right.
(26) K: No.
(27) S: All right, let's put this in a "maybe" pile. *(S puts the drawing of the egg shape on the table, then studies it.)*
(28) K: *(K touches ellipse line drawing.)* It don't look like it, looks more like this. *(K offers S ellipse line drawing. S moves stand back and forth from screen.)* There, it won't turn out like that either. *(S rotates shape on stand.)*
(29) S: Mm, here.
(30) K: We gotta trace, trace it on that *(paper screen)*. *(K picks up a pencil.)*
(31) S: Wait a minute. Is it right? *(S checks the shadow with the drawing. K watches S's shadow adjustments.)* Gotta be a little bigger. *(S rotates shape to achieve a wider ellipse.)* Since we can get it exact, we might as well.
(32) K: Here , bring it back. *(K adjusts the distance of the stand from the screen.)*
(33) K: Trace it, you can trace it. *(K offers pencil to S.)*

A few minutes later, as another elliptical shape appears on the screen, but in a vertical position, Karen proposes that they reconsider the egg shape again (line 18). Steven at first expresses his uncertainty (line 19), and Karen makes her first, clearly negative assertion about the egg (line 20). Once again the roles reverse and Steven assumes the job of shape manipulator and supporter of the plausibility of the egg-shaped hypothesis (line 21). Karen assumes the role of observer and director (lines 21 and 22). By the end of line 21, Steven makes his strongest positive assertion about the egg, "Yeah, this one works." At this point, their differing positions about that hypothesis have become solidified: Karen becomes convinced that the oval shadows that they are getting are not egg shaped, while Steven is more positive that they are.

As they continue to adjust the shadow a bit more, Karen becomes even more sure of her position. She asserts it repeatedly but does not explain herself to Steven (lines 24 and 26). Although Steven remains unconvinced by her assertions (line 25), he decides to avoid a direct confrontation by putting the egg-shaped figure aside in a pile of shadows they might be able to make (line 27). By so doing, he indirectly indicates their disagreement. Thus a compromise solution is achieved, but no real consensus is obtained.

Finally, on line 28, Karen provides some support for her position by proposing an alternative to the egg, the ellipse. Karen is so sure of herself that she suggests they trace the shadow on line 30. Steven continues to be skeptical about Karen's position (line 31). However, by the end of line 31, it is clear that Steven accepts the fact that they can make an ellipse. In lines 31 to 32, they both make some minor adjustments in the shadow so that it matches as closely as possible the line drawing, and in line 33 Karen asks Steven to trace the elliptical shadow.

What we have described in detail has been the co-construction of the hypothesis that circular shapes can produce elliptical shadows. As you have seen, this hypothesis was not present at the beginning of the session, but it emerged as a result of trying to produce an egg-shaped shadow. Initially, the two subjects' conceptions of the goal of their activities were incomplete and dissimilar. At different times, either Steven or Karen would propose that egg-shaped shadows were possible. When this occurred, their partner would assume a complementary position of observer and critic. Thus, one person tried to produce the data necessary to support the hypothesis, and the other observed and provided feedback about the fit between data and predictions. As elliptical shadows were produced, and the difference between the shadow and the egg-shaped line drawing was noted by Karen (line 16), the goal of the activity began to change for her. Although Steven was still willing to defend the egg-shaped hypothesis, Karen decided to take a negative stand against it. Between lines 16 and 26, Karen and Steven were gathering the same set of data to explore clearly different hypotheses. The reliance on data to test plausible hypotheses informally is, according to Hanson (1958), the hallmark of scientific discovery. "The critical moment comes when the physicist perceives that one might reason about the data in such and such a way. . . . The reasoning is from data to hypotheses and theories, not the reverse" (p. 88).

Hanson's account of scientific invention is quite similar to Vygotsky's (1962) and Wertsch's (1979) descriptions of the emergence of new cognitive skills. All three theorists focus on the discovery process itself, not only on its outcome. They show how the problem solver (the scientist or the child) begins working on a new task with a set of strategies and an incomplete or inadequate conception of the task goal. However, in the process of attempting to solve the task, appropriate strategies are selected and recombined in new ways, feedback from the social and nonsocial environment is incorporated into subsequent activities, and, eventually, new definitions of the task situation emerge. What both the child and the scientist gain are some metacognitive or strategic skills. For the child, of course, the strategic information is transmitted by his or her instructional partner. Scientists, working alone or in collaboration with others, need to construct or co-construct these metacognitive insights. (For an illustration of scientific collaboration, see Watson, 1968.) Although most of these changing task definitions are largely implicit, the goal of scientific discovery is to produce some plausible hypothetical statement (a principle, a formula, or an organizing pattern such as Kepler's model of elliptical planetary orbits). Hanson claims that once this principle, formula, or pattern is hypothesized, discovery is complete and verification can begin.

By lines 27 and 28, Karen manages to get Steven to abandon his hypothesis, at least for a while, and to help provide her with the data necessary to support hers. The same strategies that were originally used to produce egg-shaped shadows, that is, rotations of the circle, are redirected toward a new goal, an ellipse. By the end of line 31, it is clear that they both share an implicit situation definition concerning elliptical shadows. Steven affirms his acceptance of Karen's position that the shadows are elliptical when he says, "Since we can get it exact, we might as well."

However, Steven has not given up his hypothesis about the plausibility of egg-shaped shadows. At this point, there is a clear conflict between their two conceptions of the phenomena, which is reflected in their interaction when they reconsider the egg.

(34) S: This one *(the egg-shaped line drawing)* I think we can do. I really think we can. *(S adjusts the stand and rotates the circle.)*
(35) K: It's not going to turn out like an egg.
(36) S: If you do this you can't see what it is. *(S holds the drawing up to the screen.*
(37) K: Terrible. It's not gonna work *(said in a whisper).*
(38) S: Don't you think that's it? I don't . . .
(39) K: No. *(K laughs.)*
(40) S: Well, is it really s'posed, is it really s'posed to just be an oval or is it s'posed to be like pointed down here and . . . *(S says this to E.)*
(41) E: It's s'posed to be pointed.
(42) S: OK, then this doesn't work. *(S throws line drawing down on the table.)*

Later on during the testing phase, Steven wants to reexamine the egg because he feels it is still a plausible hypothesis (lines 34 and 38). Karen, however, is positive that it is not (lines 35, 37, and 39). This social and cognitive conflict produces a change in approach to the task. Now, each partner must defend his or her own hypothesis with data. They no longer work together to co-construct a solution to the problem. Instead, each must prove the validity of his or her own hypothesis by attending to evidence that both confirms and disconfirms it. In this way, a discovery process shifts to a verification one.

Karen's strong negative assertions about the egg-shaped hypothesis produce sufficient social conflict to alert Steven to a piece of empirical evidence he had been ignoring: the fact that the drawing was pointed on one end and the shadow was not. At this point, Steven enlists the assistance of the examiner to help him resolve his cognitive conflict. He asks her to judge the importance of the evidence that disconfirms his hypothesis (line 40). When she asserts its importance (line 41), Steven realizes that his hypothesis has not been verified by the data (line 42). Steven's recognition of this fact is demonstrated during the evaluation phase when the examiner explicitly asks them about the egg-shaped shadow ("Figure 4").

(43) E: OK. What about Figure 4?
(44) S: Figure 4?
(45) K: It's impossible. It can't be bigger on one end . . . and small at the bottom. *(K says this at the same time as S's response in line 46).*
(46) S: Well, you can almost get it except you can't get it bigger around here and smaller down here.

Both Karen and Steven provide simultaneously, the evidence that disconfirms the egg-shaped hypothesis (lines 45 and 46). Their initial predispositions about this hypothesis are still reflected in their responses: Karen emphasizes the differences between the shadow and an egg while Steven indicates the similarity between the two. The fact that both subjects more fully articulate the difference between an egg shape and an elliptical shadow than did the examiner in line 41 suggests that their consensus is not merely an imitation of the examiner's answer.

This segment of transcript illustrates that both discovery and verification can occur within the context of collaborative problem solving. Although these two processes can be distinguished conceptually, in reality the distinction is less clear since subjects seem to move from one mode of inquiry to the other in a fluid manner. This transcript provides a better example of invention than it does of verification, in part because of the nature of the shadows task and in part because the examiner answered Steven's question (line 41). If the examiner had suggested that the two partners come to a consensus about the answer, then we might have been able to observe more peer-induced logical verification.

Suggestions for Future Research

The illustration of collaborative problem solving presented here provides some support for both Piaget's and Vygotsky's theories concerning the social origins of logic. As we have seen, peer interaction can help children co-construct new solutions to problems as well as encourage them to verify solutions that conflict. This illustration suggests that an observational approach can provide valuable information about the role of peer interaction in cognitive development. However, as we have argued, the appropriate strategies, both methodological and theoretical, for observing cognition in social contexts are still being developed.

How can we improve our future research activities in this area? First, we need to identify some problem-solving contexts that can be observed and that will permit the participants to create their own social and cognitive organizing principles. Following Vygotsky's and Piaget's suggestions, tasks in which new concepts can be co-constructed or conflicting concepts can be coordinated are the most likely settings in which to see peer interaction influence thought.

Second, we need to observe and record joint cognitive activity over time. Repeated observations of the same participants working on the same or similar tasks provide the wealth of data that is necessary if one wants to study developmental processes. This analysis can be microgenetic (Wertsch and Stone, 1978) or ontogenetic (Kuhn and Phelps, 1979) in nature. The preferred research design may be the single-subject study with replications (see Forman and Cazden, in press.)

Third, we need to change the ways in which we code and analyze observational data. Most systematic observational coding systems rely on "bottom-up" procedures and are based on an implicit mechanistic theoretical model (Forman, 1983). Peer interaction, for example, is seen as consisting of strings of simple, discrete, individual acts. These acts are largely identified and coded irrespective of context. This model of behavior is analytic in nature: Elementary units or acts are presumed, and systems or patterns of units must be derived. Regular or predictable patterns among acts (for example, smiling follows mutual eye contact more often than would be predicted by chance) form the large systems or patterns of units.

However, a bottom-up approach does not provide meaningful information about cognitive processes. In cognition, any individual behavioral act can serve a multitude of functions, depending upon the context in which it occurs. For example, scanning an array of materials could indicate that a subject is planning his or her next activity if it occurs after the previous activity is completed. If, however, scanning interrupts ongoing activity, it might suggest an inability to maintain attention to the task. The context-dependency of behavioral acts in cognitive activity suggests a "top-down" approach instead. A top-down approach would view joint cognitive activity as consisting of complex, interconnected activity systems. This model would be synthetic: Wholes or activity systems are assumed, and individual acts must be derived. In addition, individual acts would be defined by the context in which they are embedded. This approach is derived from an organismic or contextualistic model. One way to implement a top-down procedure would be to use a task that is structured like the shadows task, as a sequence of recurring phases. Then the stream of behavior can be segmented into episodes defined by subjects' activity, not by time or behavioral acts.

We plan to use some of these ideas in subsequent analyses of the data we have collected on peer collaboration in the shadows task. We are, at present, evaluating the problem-attack and reasoning strategies used by the subjects in this study. We plan to augment this analysis with an examination of their social strategies (for example, co-construction versus social conflict). Both of these analyses will be implemented for each of the six shapes presented so that microgenetic change within and across sessions can be documented. In addition, we plan to trace the genesis of qualitatively different understandings of the task. This analysis will be done by locating segments of the transcript from a particular pair of subjects that deal with a concept or set of metacognitive procedures. For example, one could examine how two subjects come to a common understanding of some of the general principles that govern the projection of shadows of geometric shapes (for instance, the conditions under which symmetric relations or parallelisms are preserved). One could see how these principles are co-constructed, initially, to serve pragmatic ends and when they are modified in response to disconfirming social or nonsocial feedback.

Finally, we need to be willing to revise the "in the head" view of cognition. Doise and his colleagues have made an initial step in this direction by calling their work social constructivism in order to emphasize "the chain or circular (or spiral) causality which connects cognitive functions with the interpersonal interactions in which the child participates" (Mugny and others, 1981, pp. 315-316).

References

Bearison, D. J. "New Directions in Studies of Social Interaction and Cognitive Growth." In F. C. Serafica (Ed.), *Social Cognitive Development in Context*. New York: Guilford, 1982.

Clements, M. A., and Wattanawaha, N. *Monash Space Visualization Test*. Melbourne, Australia: Monash University, 1978.

Doise, W., and Mackie, D. "On the Social Nature of Cognition." In J. P. Forgas (Ed.), *Social Cognition*. New York: Academic Press, 1981.

Doise, W., Mugny, G., and Perret-Clermont, A.-N. "Social Interaction and the Development of Cognitive Operations." *European Journal of Social Psychology*, 1975, 5 (3), 367-383.

Doise, W., Mugny, G., and Perret-Clermont, A.-N. "Social Interaction and Cognitive Development: Further Evidence." *European Journal of Social Psychology*, 1976, 6, 245-247.

Emler, N., and Valiant, G. L. "Social Interaction and Cognitive Conflict in the Development of Spatial Coordination Skills." *British Journal of Psychology*, 1982, 73, 295-303.

Forman, E. A. "The Role of Collaboration in Problem-Solving in Children." Unpublished doctoral dissertation, Harvard University, 1981.

Forman, E. A. "The Role of Developmental Models in the Study of Children's Social Interaction." Paper presented at the biennial meeting of the Society for Research in Child Development, Detroit, April 1983.

Forman, E. A., and Cazden, C. B. "Exploring Vygotskian Perspectives in Education: The Cognitive Value of Peer Interaction." In J. V. Wertsch (Ed.), *Culture, Communication, and Cognition: Vygotskian Perspectives*. New York: Cambridge University Press (in press).

Glachan, M., and Light, P. "Peer Interaction and Learning: Can Two Wrongs Make a Right?" In G. Butterworth and P. Light (Eds.), *Social Cognition: Studies of the Development of Understanding*. Chicago: University of Chicago Press, 1982.

Hanson, N. R. *Patterns of Discovery: An Inquiry into the Conceptual Foundation of Science*. Cambridge, England: Cambridge University Press, 1958.

Kuhn, D. "Mechanisms of Cognitive and Social Development: One Psychology or Two?" *Human Development*, 1978, *21*, 92-118.

Kuhn, D., and Phelps, E. "A Methodology for Observing Development of a Formal Reasoning Strategy." In D. Kuhn (Ed.), *Intellectual Development Beyond Childhood*. New Directions for Child Development, no. 5. San Francisco: Jossey-Bass, 1979.

Kuhn, D., and Phelps, E. "The Development of Problem-Solving Strategies." In H. Reese and L. Lipsitt (Eds.), *Advances in Child Development and Behavior*. Vol. 17. New York: Academic Press, 1982.

Mead, G. H. *Mind, Self, and Society*. Chicago: University of Chicago Press, 1934.

Mugny, G., Perret-Clermont, A.-N., and Doise, W. "Interpersonal Coordinations and Sociological Differences in the Construction of the Intellect." In G. M. Stephenson and J. M. Davis (Eds.), *Progress in Applied Social Psychology*. Vol. 1. New York: Wiley, 1981.

Overton, W. F., and Reese, H. W. "Models of Development: Methodological Indications." In J. Nesselroade and H. Reese (Eds.), *Life-Span Developmental Psychology: Methodological Issues*. New York: Academic Press, 1973.

Pepper, S. C. *World Hypotheses*. Berkeley: University of California Press, 1942.

Perret-Clermont, A.-N. *Social Interaction and Cognitive Development in Children*. New York: Academic Press, 1980.

Piaget, J. *The Language and Thought of the Child*. London: Routledge & Kegan Paul, 1926.

Piaget, J. *Judgment and Reasoning in the Child*. London: Routledge & Kegan Paul, 1928.

Piaget, J. *The Psychology of Intelligence*. London: Routledge & Kegan Paul, 1950.

Piaget, J. *The Moral Judgment of the Child*. New York: Free Press, 1965.

Stone, C. A., Forman, E. A., and Anderson, C. J. "Delay Versus Difference in Cognitive Development: A Comparison of Learning-Disabled Adolescents and Two Normal Achieving Groups in an Isolation of Variables Task." Paper presented at the Fifth International Conference on Learning Disabilities, San Francisco, October 1983.

Tisher, R. P. "A Piagetian Questionnaire Applied to Pupils in a Secondary School." *Child Development*, 1971, *42*, 1633-1636.

Vygotsky, L. S. *Thought and Language*. Cambridge, Mass.: M.I.T. Press, 1962.

Vygotsky, L. S. *Mind in Society*. Cambridge, Mass.: Harvard University Press, 1978.

Watson, J. D. *The Double Helix*. New York: New American Library, 1968.

Wertsch, J. V. "From Social Interaction to Higher Psychological Processes: A Clarification and Application of Vygotsky's Theory." *Human Development*, 1979, *22*, 3-22.

Wertsch, J. V., McNamee, G. D., McLane, J. B., and Budwig, N. A. "The Adult-Child Dyad as a Problem-Solving System." *Child Development*, 1980, *51*, 1215-1221.

Wertsch, J. V., and Stone, C. A. "Microgenesis as a Tool for Developmental Analysis." *Quarterly Newsletter of the Laboratory of Comparative Human Cognition*, 1978, *1* (1), 8-10.

Ellice A. Forman is assistant professor of learning disabilities, Northwestern University.

Myra J. Kraker is a doctoral student in the learning disabilities program, Northwestern University.

*The child's attempts to overcome sociocognitive
conflict, under certain specific cognitive and social
conditions, can lead to a restructuring of the child's
thinking on a supraordinate level.*

Sociocognitive Conflict and Intellectual Growth

*Nancy Bell, Michèle Grossen,
Anne-Nelly Perret-Clermont*

Many authors in different domains of psychology (developmental, epistemological, psychoanalytical) have studied the developmental consequences of *conflict,* conceiving conflict as a nonlinear process bound to different types of vicissitudes that the individual has to confront and surpass. In psychoanalytical theory, for example, conflict is seen as being constitutive to the individual's psychic being. Freudian theory of affective development emphasizes the central role played by the conflict between the pleasure and the reality principles in early childhood and its effects on the child's personality and adaptation to his or her environment. For Piaget, the notion of conflict is essential to the understanding of the child's progression through different stages of cognitive development. Epistemological studies, such as that of Inhelder and others (1974), have shown how cognitive

This article has been written with the support of Fonds National de la Recherche Scientifique, contract number 1.738-0.83. The authors' names have been listed in alphabetical order to indicate their equal contribution.

conflict can be induced by the presentation of a model of reasoning that is incongruent with the cognitive schemes of the child and how this conflict can lead to cognitive growth by provoking the reorganization of the subject's cognitive schemes in a superordinate system.

What are the sources of such conflict that promote cognitive growth? Our hypothesis is that the origins of cognitive conflict are to be found not only within the individual and his or her physical environment but in his or her social environment as well. We will argue that it is through the child's interaction with other individuals (peers as well as adults) that the child is exposed to differing cognitive strategies, and this exposure triggers active reconstruction of the child's cognitions. We have contributed to a series of research studies undertaken in the last decade that have illustrated this sociointeractive approach to studying the social origins of cognitive development. These studies have focused primarily on the process of *sociocognitive conflict* whereby the subject comes to reorganize and restructure cognitions as a result of confrontation with opposing points of view during social interaction. We suggest that the origin of developmental progress can be found in the subject's attempt to surmount the sociocognitive conflicts that arise when he or she encounters persons displaying different perspectives but with whom the subject still feels the need for a common understanding or joint action.

Sociocognitive conflict can be induced experimentally as described in the first part of this chapter, which cites several primary results from studies exploring the conditions of emergence of sociocognitive conflict. Then we will elaborate a social-psychological analysis of this phenomenon by examining first the *cognitive* and then the *social* factors that play a role in the cognitive conflict resulting in learning and intellectual growth. Let us note here that our isolation of cognitive and social factors should be understood as merely heuristic. In fact, the subsequent developmental progress is the result of *both* cognitive and social growth, brought about by the subject's need to find the means to overcome difficulties in the interpersonal coordination of action, speech, and thought.

The studies that we will present first have focused on sociocognitive conflict as created in experimental interaction sessions. But in fact any encounter (for example, a testing situation) can induce sociocognitive conflicts. Further research has shown that the emergence of such conflicts will depend on the subject's perceptions of the situation, task, partners, purpose of the interaction, and so on. Hence, we will turn to the consideration of these factors, in the later part of the chapter, when we analyze the testing situation as a *social event* wherein sociocognitive conflicts can also occur.

Experimental Results Concerning the Developmental Effects of Sociocognitive Conflict

Before presenting our results, let us first describe the experimental procedure. The basic experimental paradigm used in most of the research on sociocognitive conflict employs three steps consisting of a pretest, an experimental interaction session, and a posttest. The experimental tasks have primarily been Piagetian operatory tasks (that is, tests of conservcation of liquid, substance, number and so on) although other tasks have been used (such as tasks of motor coordination and drawing). These tasks are intended for subjects ranging from four to seven years of age (with the age of experimental subjects depending on the age of the acquisition of the particular notion under study). Let us briefly describe the experimental procedure using the conservation of liquid as an example:

1. *Pretest:* The conservation of liquid test is administered individually to each subject using a clinical (semi-directive) interview requiring different conservation judgments with accompanying justifications. The aim of the pretest is to ascertain the child's operatory level.

2. *Interaction Session:* One week later, each nonconserving child is paired with either another nonconserver or a conserving child in order to "play a game" whose aim is the sharing of an equal quantity of juice. The experimenter gives one child a glass that is taller and thinner than the other child's glass and tells the nonconserving child to pour the same amount of juice for him- or herself and the partner. (A third glass, identical to the second glass is at the children's disposal and may also be used). More often than not, the nonconserving child pours the juice to the same level in both glasses, which elicits disagreement from the partner. The "game" ends when the two children agree that they both have the same amount to drink.

3. *Posttest:* After one week, the nonconserving subjects are retested individually on the conservation of liquid tests and parallel generalization tasks.

Experimental results using this three-step paradigm (reported in Doise and others, 1975; Perret-Clermont, 1980; and Perret-Clermont and Schubauer-Leoni, 1981) indicate that, under certain circumstances, subjects who participate in the interaction session display more cognitive progress on the posttest than subjects in a control group who do not interact with a peer. Other studies using different tasks, such as number and length conservation, spatial transformation, and motor coordination tasks (Ames and Murray, 1982; Carugati and others, 1979; Doise and Mugny, 1981; Glachan and Light, 1981; Levy, 1981; Mackie, 1980; Perret-Clermont, 1980) have repeatedly confirmed these findings, suggesting the importance of social confrontations whereby the nonconserving child is led to *restructure* his or her reasoning as a consequence of the conflict that emerges between his or her point of view and the differing point of view of the partner in a situation where a common agreement or a joint action is required. The child is faced with a point of view seemingly incompatible to his or her own, which necessitates a cognitive restructuring in order to render the two viewpoints compatible when their coordination is demanded by the situation. The child thereby comes to see his or her own centration differently.

viewpoints compatible when their coordination is demanded by the situation. The child thereby comes to see his or her own centration differently. (We use the word *centration* in the Piagetian sense as elementary cognitive schemas that have to be coordinated into more complex structures in order to allow more advanced thinking.) The consequent cognitive reorganization and restructuring can be seen as the product of the subject's new coordinations which result from the coordination of the conflicting centrations.

Empirical evidence of profound cognitive restructuring subsequent to such conflicts is the child's ability to generalize his or her newly acquired conservation judgments to other tasks—for instance, from the concept of the conservation of liquid to other types of conservation, such as the conservation of matter or length. Results regularly have confirmed the hypothesis according to which the cognitive restructuring following an interaction session is observable not only on the task dealt with during the interaction but also on new tasks unfamiliar to the child.

Cognitive Analysis of Sociocognitive Conflict

Imitation or Confrontation? If one analyzes the phenomenon of sociocognitive conflict from a cognitive perspective, one of the first questions that comes to mind concerns the nature of the progress observed after social interaction: Is the child simply repeating or imitating the correct response of his or her partner, or do subjects' posttest performances represent a more general and profound restructuring of cognitions? In other words, is the presentation of a correct model (or answer) a necessary condition for sociocognitive conflict and consequent cognitive growth? Mugny and others (1975-1976) examined these questions in an experiment using two conditions for the interaction session: In the first condition, the experimenter proposes an opposing but incorrect argument to the nonconserving child; in the second condition, the experimenter counterposes the child's incorrect response with the correct conserving argument. Both experimental conditions resulted in significant cognitive progress as compared to the control condition where no conflict was created. Similar results were found in other experiments involving the drawing of geometrical figures (Perret-Clermont, 1980) and spatial transformations (Doise and Mugny, 1981; Levy, 1981), in which, under certain circumstances, children benefited developmentally from social interactions with peers who were less cognitively advanced than themselves. Thus, the presentation of a correct model to the nonconserving child during the interaction session is not a necessary condition and cannot, in itself, explain the cognitive evolution observed from the pretest to the posttest. It thus appears that a confrontation between opposing cognitions can lead to a cognitive restructuring and eventually to a superior cognitive level *even if the information provoking the conflict is incorrect.* Furthermore, during the posttest, former nonconservers who interact with conserving partners do not merely repeat the arguments they have heard from their conserving partners, but they often give new and original justifications that they had not been capable of elaborating in the pretest (Perret-Clermont, 1980). Thus, progress observed after social interaction cannot be equated simply with the performance of the better of the partners.

The results of the research just cited converge in suggesting that an important criterion for cognitive progress is that conflict should be socially present. A subject faced with an interaction partner holding a viewpoint similar to his or her own will lack exposure to contradictory perspectives, and such exposure is essential to cognitive restructuring and progress. For example, we have observed nonconserving children quickly come to an agreement, both seemingly unperturbed by the fact that they have established equal levels of juice in two differently shaped glasses! Thus, attempts at cooperative problem solving are not sufficient for the interpersonal interaction to have an effect. Cognitive progress only results from sociocognitive conflict when partners' respective viewpoints are opposed and in need of coordination.

Cognitive "Prerequisites." Although significant cognitive progress can be observed in children after participation in an interaction session, the fact remains that not all children benefit from such a situation. Results show that subjects who have not yet understood basic notions underlying the problem at hand are less likely to progress following the interaction session. For example, Perret-Clermont and Schubauer-Leoni (1981) found that those subjects who did not demonstrate the notion of renversabilité on the conservation of liquid test did not progress at all on the posttest. (*Renversabilité* is a French term indicating, in this context, that the child believes that when the juice is poured back into the identical glasses it has somehow been transformed and will not be the same amount.) Concerning the conservation of number, Perret-Clermont (1980) observed that only those subjects who already performed at one of the higher levels of nonconservation on the pretest were able to benefit from the social interaction so that their posttest performance showed cognitive restructuring. In order that sociocognitive conflict has developmental consequences, the child needs to have attained a minimum level of task mastery (that is, to possess certain cognitive "prerequisites"), a level that allows the child to understand the problem and to play an active part in the discussion and confrontation. If the child does not comprehend the task or is incapable of perceiving the incompatibility of differing centrations, no conflict will ensue. Such an encounter evidently will have no developmental effect for the child. In fact, if the child lacks the necessary prerequisites, neither interindividual nor individual activity will enable the child to progress (Mugny and others, 1981).

Forms of Conflict: The Role of the Partner's Cognitive Level. Will the confrontation of an opposing strategy automatically have cognitive benefits for the subject, or does the partner's cognitive level play an important role in the emergence of conflict-induced cognitive progress? Studies by Kuhn (1972) suggest that there is an optimal gap between the subject's developmental level and that of a social model. This gap should be small enough so that the difference in behaviors corresponds to the acquisition the child has to make and large enough so that the contradiction between the two sets of behaviors produces cognitive disequilibrium.

Mugny and Doise (1978) explored forms of socioconflicts that could facilitate cognitive progress by manipulating the partner's cognitive level. They examined the collective performance of dyads on a spatial transformation task—specifically, the "three mountains" task (Piaget and others, 1948).

The composition of the dyads was varied as a function of individual performance on the pretest (where subjects were ranked on low, intermediate, and advanced levels). Results show that, when low-level subjects work together with advanced-level subjects, they do not display cognitive progress on the posttest *even though* they solve the task during the interaction session. This "resolution of conflict" is usually achieved by the imposition of a solution by the advanced subject, thereby eliminating the opportunity for the low-level subject to coordinate his or her approach with that of the advanced partner. Low-level subjects who interacted with another low-level subject likewise showed little progress on the posttest as both tended to use the same problem-solving strategy, thus excluding the possibility of the emergence of conflict.

On the other hand, when the low-level subject is paired with an intermediate subject, the characteristics of the interaction are different: "The intermediate subject, whose system is less stable, is perturbed by the unacceptable solution proposed by the low subject, although he does not yet possess the cognitive instruments necessary to solve the problem. While looking for a satisfactory solution, the intermediate subjects explicate their strategy and the problems they face. As a result, they progress, but so do the low-level subjects who are able to take part in the search for a correct solution" (Mugny and Doise, 1978). Such a confrontation serves to make each partner aware of the existence of alternate solutions, which enhances the possibility of both partners modifying their own solution as they realize its insufficiency. Thus, neither child remains unchanged by the social interaction.

Is Conflict Resolution Necessary for Cognitive Growth? The research presented so far suggests that the important element in sociocognitive conflict is the conflictual aspect of the interaction and not necessarily its resolution. In our research, we have been able to enumerate many different strategies for conflict resolution; however, we have found that the dynamic that occurs between children during the interaction session is not necessarily predictive of the agreement reached at the end of the session or of the posttest results. We have not yet discovered any direct causal link between the type of conflict resolution achieved and the level of cognitive progress displayed on the posttest. Analyses of our results indicate that, although conflict resolution can lead to cognitive progress, it is *not* a necessary condition for cognitive restructuring and development.

Conflict resolution during social interaction can in fact prevent the child from progressing beyond his or her initial pretest performance. This was the case in the experiment of Mugny and Doise (1978), cited earlier, where subjects did not progress even though the correct solution had been elaborated during the interaction session, due to the imposition of a solution by the advanced partner. Likewise, Mugny and others (1979) found that subjects who systematically resolved conflict by accepting the contradictory responses of their partner (an adult in this casee) did not demonstrate any cognitive progress.

Social Factors in Sociocognitive Conflict

Up to this point we have regarded the child as essentially "generic" with no consideration of specific social characteristics liable to influence cognitive development. However, since sociocognitive conflicts are products of interactions that do not take place in a social vacuum, it is not reasonable to abstract the individual either from interpersonal interactions, which are constitutive of the individual's cognitive mechanisms, or from social background and social group memberships, which play an influential role in behavior. Although cognitive functioning has been seen traditionally as an intraindividual phenomenon, it seems evident to us that it cannot be examined independent of its social context.

Hence we will now look briefly at the occurrence of sociocognitive conflict for subjects belonging to different social groups. We have often observed (Mugny and others, 1981; Perret-Clermont, 1980; Perret-Clermont and Schubauer-Leoni, 1981) a correlation between pretest performance and social category membership, with children from advantaged backgrounds showing significantly higher operatory levels than their disadvantaged peers (an observation often corroborated by results from other cognitive tests). We were thus particularly interested in the amount of progress evidenced by disadvantaged children subsequent to social interaction. Systematic analysis of results by social group has shown that the socioeconomic differences observed on the pretest tend, for the most part, to diminish on the posttest. It is as if the social interaction gave disadvantaged subjects the opportunity more or less to "catch up" with their more cognitively advanced, economically advantaged peers. Thus, we can no longer speak of inherent "socioeconomic or cultural handicaps" if, under certain circumstances, we can reduce these so-called handicaps by a five-to-ten minute experimental session.

These results have led us to investigate the relation between social category membership and the testing situation in which cognitive development is elicited. Perret-Clermont and Schubauer-Leoni (1981) specifically studied the effect of task presentation on children's responses using the three-step design. In the pretest, two conditions were presented: In the first condition, the Piagetian conservation of liquid task was administered in such a way that the child had to share the juice equally with the experimenter. In the second condition, the child had to give equal amounts of juice to two identical dolls. Pretest results indicate that the presentation of the experimental task had a notable effect on certain social groups: Girls and disadvantaged children seem to be particularly sensitive to this variable, performing more poorly in the test with the dolls. However, these differences disappeared after the experimental interaction session. The observed pretest differences can be taken as indicating that subjects are not faced with the same relation situation, even if it is standardized rigorously in the eyes of the experimenter. Their perception of the situation affects their elaboration of a cognitive competence.

The fact that cognitive performance for certain social groups can vary as a function of task presentation suggests that it is not only individual psychological competencies that are important here but also (and perhaps above all) social ones (such as the ability to establish a certain type of discourse in relation to a given object with a socially defined interlocutor in a given situation). Subjects come to the experimental situation with a wide range of past experience (cognitive "prerequisites," social and relational experience, and so on). These experiential factors will modify the subjects' interpretation of the testing situation and (consequently) their behavior in such a situation.

Further exploration of the effects of the social variables and the relational processes at work in the actualization of an operatory notion is needed. In the following section we will consider both the interaction session *and* the testing situations (pretest and posttest) as *social events* in which sociocognitive conflicts take place. It is important to note here that any situation in which the child interacts with another person (be it child or adult) is potentially conflictual. The "individual" testing situation is in fact a complex social interaction. Although the social dynamics of this particular situation are often ignored by traditional psychological analysis, the basic interactional processes are comparable (if not the same) to the more "prototypical" social interaction session. Both contexts are rational settings that require cognitive as well as social skills from their participants.

The Testing Situation as a Social Event

In interactions in which sociocognitive conflict takes place, the participants not only have to activate the cognitions necessary to solve the problem at hand, but they also have to rely on or elaborate the social knowledge that is essential to the comprehension of the interaction. A sociocognitive conflict can only occur if the context and the object of the interactaion are mutually understood by the partners.

Essential to the mutual understanding of the interaction is the sharing of the same implicit assumptions about the situation. Thus, meaningful discourse has as its prerequisite the development of an "intersubjectivity"—that is, a shared social reality that is congruent to the participants. In order for the partners to make sense of an interaction, they need to establish a shared frame of reference, which will permit the development of a tacitly assumed commonality with respect to interpretation of each participant's utterances (see Rommetveit, 1979). However, as Rommetveit suggests, one of the important features of adult-child interaction is the fact that "this relation is asymmetric in the sense that the [adult], and he alone by virtue of his role, is fully in control of the premises for interpretation and the criteria by which comprehension and intersubjectivity are evaluated" (p. 12).

In our experimental paradigm, this means that one of the conditions of successful participation in the interaction session is the acceptance of the premises imposed by the adult experimenter, which implies making sense of what is going on. This does not necessarily preclude eventual negotiation (which could provoke conflict and hence be seen as part of the learning process that already occurs during the pretest), but it does mean that, faced with a Piagetian task for the first time, the child's primary task is to try to decode the tacit assumptions of the adult concerning the definition of the situation, the expected roles, the focus of the discussion, and the "taken for granted" aspects of the interaction. All of these are necessary in order for the child to answer the demands of the experimenter, to engage in a sociocognitive conflict, and to benefit from its developmental impact. Let us now analyze the conservation of liquid task from the *child's* viewpoint in order to understand better what social knowledge is required to interpret the adult's discourse and hence to succeed at the task.

Perception of the Experimental Situation and of the Task. The probability of the occurrence of sociocognitive conflict will depend, in large part, on the way in which the partners perceive and comprehend the experimental task and situation, which in turn allows them to enter into discussion of the object of debate as expected by the experimenter. For this reason we will now examine the experimental situation, focusing on the pretest, since it figures predominantly in the child's initial attempts to make sense of the situation and to elaborate a response (which will then be taken by the adult as an indication of the child's cognitive level).

In our pretests, as with many experiments, the experimental interaction begins with an unknown (or relatively unknown) adult interrupting the child's classroom activity to remove him or her from a habitual context with the justification that "we are going to play a game together." This game, as it turns out, has few features in common with any game the child is familiar with. In effect, this "game" resembles to a great degree a testing or examination situation where the adult asks a number of questions to which he or she already knows the response and to which the child is obliged to give answers as well as justifications of these answers. In some respects, the whole situation could look very ambiguous.

As we can see, the definition of the situation imposed by the adult will serve to structure the subsequent interaction. The child will modulate his or her social expectations according to his or her representation of the situation: On being told they are going to "play a game," the child could be led to expect an enjoyable activity, which, perhaps, would have a set of rules, where partners take turns, and so on. One could hypothesize here that a mismatch between the child's anticipated representation of a "game" and what the adult defines as a "game" could hinder the subject's chances to answer correctly.

When confronted by such a situation, the child has to rely primarily on implicit cues (such as the experimenter's voice intonation, body and facial gestures, and other cues embedded in the situation) in order to apprehend that he or she is not intended, in fact, to play a real game but to consider a problem. During the course of the experiment, the dialogue will provide the child with more cues that allow the child to decode the experimenter's precise (although implicit) expectations and help to construct the social significance of the interaction. The child's interpretation of the goals of the experimenter and the successful culmination of the interrogation (that it is not a matter of winning the game in the usual sense and that the purpose of the adult's questioning is evalutive rather than lucid) could determine the quality of the responses.

The subject must also perceive the problem as essentially cognitive and not relational or affective. The social interaction (between adult and child in this context) could elicit a cognitive conflict but concerning another object than the operatory problem proposed by the adult, which would reduce the subject's chances of attaining a higher operatory level. The importance of the child's entering into the pretest discussion on a *cognitive* plane could have eventual repercussions on the social interaction session between children where a sociocognitive conflict must be apprehended as such by the participants. If the conflict becomes relational or affective or if it is resolved on a plane other than cognitive, the conflict will not always have the intended effect on the child's operatory development.

An important feature in the perception of the situation is the comprehension of the task. The material manipulated by the experimenter (and the child) plays an essential role by providing visual cues to which the child can refer. However, the child must be able to discern which aspects of the material are relevant to the solving of the task. In the conservation of liquid task, the child has to understand that the kind of liquid used and the different dimensions of the glasses are *not* pertinent cues to the resolution of the problem, despite the multiple manipulations by the experimenter. In other words, the child must not only understand what the discussion is about but also what it is *not* about! Despite the perceptual evidence displayed, the experimenter actually is interested in the quantity of juice and not in the level of the juice or in the pouring and drinking of juice. Thus, the more obvious social cues in this situation are, in reality, the very ones that the child must ignore. In order to reach an advanced developmental level in an operatory task, the child has to realize that the perceptual transformation that occurs after each pouring and that seems to have a certain importance (as indicated by the questioning it provokes from the experimenter) is precisely the point not to take into consideration when answering!

The type of material utilized in a task can likewise enhance or inhibit the child's cognitive performance. The presupposition of the conservation of liquid task is that the child should not associate the elements of this new situation with any previous experience.

Social Relations in the Testing Situation. The interpersonal situation in which a cognitive response is solicited from the subject is not only influenced by his or her perception of the task and context but also by the kind of social relations existing between the interactants and by the particular expectations associated with these relations.

In the liquid conservation task, the child is told by the adult to pour an equal quantity of juice for each of them. In light of the social relation existing between the two participants, this request could strike the child as aberrant, given the fact that adults and children are not equal in respect to their social and physical status. In order to become a conserver, the child must come to realize that the physical and social status of the partners are not relevant to the task. The child must abstract the problem from the embedded social relations in the testing situation.

In the research of Perret-Clermont and Schubauer-Leoni (1981), the observation that girls gave conserving judgments more often when they had to share the juice between the experimenter and themselves than when the juice was divided up for two dolls could be explained (partiallly) by the supposition that it was easier for them to abstract from an actual social relationship than from a "let's pretend" pretext embedded within the testing situation. The "dolls" condition seems to demand more abstraction as the child effectively must understand that the point of the "game" is the equal sharing of the juice and not playing with dolls.

Expectations of Role and Episode. The conservation of liquid task considered as a social event can be analyzed in terms of the expectations the interactants hold concerning their respective roles and the script of the episode. Faced with a novel situation, the child is likely to refer to similar previous interactions in order to orient his or her behavior. School children very probably have developed elaborate schemes of conduct or scripts for adult-child interactions in a scholastic context and consequently come to this situation with certain preconceived notions of how the adult will behave, how the child must act, and so on.

The child's perception of the roles of the social episode and of the adult's expectations play a crucial part in attempts to solve the task. Through the course of the interaction, the child will be led to choose which aspects of the situation are pertinent to task resolution and which dimensions of the task to abstract from. These will be a function of his or her perception and interpretation of the adult's reactions. This "cueing" will not only determine the child's elaboration of the response in the testing situation but will also provide the basis upon which the child can enter into a sociocognitive conflict.

Summary. In this section we have analyzed the testing situation as a social event comprised of a complex set of elements potentially determinant of the subject's behaviors. One could say that the child's cognitive performance is a product of the social interaction taking place within this situation. In order to enter into the discussion, to display a competency successfully, and eventually to perceive the conflicting position of one's partners during the social interaction, the child must apprehend the definition of the situation and the script of the episode. The child must also accurately perceive the adult's expectations of the partners' respective roles as well as the aim and purpose of the discussion (as it relates to the task material at hand and so on).

The fact that children from advantaged backgrounds show a higher operatory level on Piagetian operatory pretests than disadvantaged children can be reinterpreted in the light of this perspective. It seems that, at a given age, children of high socioeconomic status understand more quickly the social "implicits" (roles, expectations, and so forth) embedded in this particular situation. It is as if they can distance themselves more easily from the normative script and role expectations that are implied by the school context and that are not entirely applicable to the experimental episode. However, given appropriate conditions of social interaction (which permit a better understanding of such a situation), children from disadvantaged backgrounds can "recover," showing posttest performances equal to their privileged peers.

Conclusions

What are the sources of conflict that can promote intellectual growth? As we have seen, the individual's social environment, besides the physical environment, offers important occasions for interactional confrontations of opposing cognitions. The child's attempts to overcome sociocognitive conflict can lead to a restructuring of his or her thinking on a superordinate level. We have put forth evidence to show that this restructuring is not simply the consequence of imitation but of real conflict. In order that sociocognitive conflict be productive, certain cognitive *as well as* social conditions need to be fulfilled. The child must possess not only the right cognitive prerequisites for task resolution but also must manage to decipher the social situation.

At this point we suggest that social interaction between peers not only provides the subject with the opportunity to confront his or her response with that of another but also provides the occasion to abstract the pertinent dimensions from the social situation enabling him or her to solve the problem. Thus, a sociocognitive conflict promotes cognitive *and* social growth. By responding to the social demands of the situation, the child comes to elaborate a social knowledge leading to new frames of understanding. In this perspective, the cognitive progress displayed following conflict can be seen as a product of the complex interplay between the social and cognitive dimensions of the interaction.

References

Ames, G. J., and Murray, F. "When Two Wrongs Make a Right: Provoking Cognitive Change by Social Conflict." *Developmental Psychology*, 1982, *18* (6), 894-897.

Carugati, F., De Paolis, P., and Mugny, G. "A Paradigm for the Study of Social Interactions in Cognitive Development."*Italian Journal of Psychology*, 1979, *6*, 147-155.

Doise, W., and Mugny, G. *Le Développement social de l'intelligence.* Paris: Interéditions, 1981.

Doise, W., Mugny, G. and Perret-Clermont, A.-N. "Social Interaction and the Development of Cognitive Operations." *European Journal of Social Psychology*, 1975, *5*, 367-383.

Glachan, M., and Light, P. "Peer Interaction and Learning: Can Two Wrongs Make a Right?" In G. Butterworth and P. Light (Eds.), *Social Cognition: Studies in the Development of Understanding.* Brighton, England: Harvester Press, October 1981.

Inhelder, B., Sinclair, H., and Bovet, M. *Apprentissage et structures de la connaissance.* Paris: Presse Universitaire de France, 1974.

Kuhn, D. "Mechanism of Change in the Development of Cognitive Structures." *Child Development*, 1972, *43*, 833-844.

Levy, M. "La nécessité sociale de dépasser une situation conflictuelle générée par la presentation d'un modèle de solution de problème et par le questionnement d'un agent social." Unpublished doctoral dissertation, University of Geneva, 1981.

Mackie, D. "A Cross-Cultural Study of Intraindividual and Interindividual Conflicts of Centration." *European Journal of Social Psychology*, 1980, *10*, 313-318.

Mugny, G., and Doise, W. "Sociocognitive Conflict and Structuration of Individual and Collective Performances." *European Journal of Social Psychology*, 1978, *8*, 181-192.

Mugny, G., Doise, W., and Perret-Clermont, A.-N. "Conflict de centrations et progrès cognitif." *Bulletin de Psychologie*, 1975-76, *29*, 199-204.

Mugny, G., Giroud, J., and Doise, W. "Conflict de centration et progrès cognitif." *Bulletin de Psychologie*, 1979, *32*, 978-985.

Mugny, G., Perret-Clermont, A.-N. and Doise, W. "Interpersonal Coordinations and Sociological Differences in the Construction of the Intellect." In G. M. Stephenson and J. M. Davis (Eds.), *Progress in Applied Social Psychology.* Vol. 1. New York: Wiley, 1981.

Perret-Clermont, A.-N. *Social Interaction and Cognitive Development in Children.* London: Academic Press, 1980.

Perret-Clermont, A.-N., and Schubauer-Leoni, M. L. "Conflict and Cooperation as Opportunities for Learning." In W. P. Robinson (Ed.), *Communication in Development.* London: Academic Press, 1981.

Piaget, J., Inhelder, B. and Szeminska, A. *La Géométrie spontanée chez l'enfant.* Paris: Presse Universitaire de France, 1948.

Rommetveit, R. "On Common Codes and Dynamic Residuals in Human Communication." In R. M. Blakar and R. Rommetveit (Eds.), *Studies of Language, Thought and Verbal Communication.* London: Academic Press, 1979.

Nancy Bell is a researcher at the University of Neuchâtel and the University of Geneva, Switzerland.

Michèle Grossen is a researcher at the University of Neuchâtel and the University of Geneva, Switzerland.

Anne-Nelly Perret-Clermont is a professor of psychology at the University of Neuchâtel and a professor of social psychology of education at the University of Geneva, Switzerland.

Observations of naturally occurring social transgressions indicate that peer interactions in the context of moral conflicts differ qualitatively from those in the context of breaches of convention.

Social Conflict and the Development of Children's Moral and Conventional Concepts

Larry Nucci

Few developmental researchers, if any, would study children's resolution of arithmetic problems as a way of examining the sources and forms of cognitive conflict that lead to moral growth. This is because it is apparent to most researchers that although mathematical reasoning may be employed to generate informaton important to resolving moral questions (Hook, 1982), arithmetic and morality pose qualitatively differing classes of problems and are understood within correspondingly differing conceptual systems. It has been less apparent to researchers, however, that the sources of cognitive conflict that lead to moral growth differ from those that lead to conceptions of other social norms. Prevailing theories of moral development have either characterized morality as equivalent to adherence to society's values (Aronfreed, 1968; Durkheim, 1961; Hogan, 1973) or have posited an ontogenetic sequence in which at early developmental stages morality is undifferentiated from nonmoral (such as conventional or prudential) bases for social conduct (Piaget, 1932; Kohlberg, 1981). As a consequence, most research efforts aimed at identifying social experiences associated with children's moral development have not differentiated those aspects that are particular to the development of morality from those associated with the development of the child's understandings of other forms of social or personal regulation.

Over the past decade, however, a considerable amount of research has provided findings indicating that children's conceptions of morality are distinct from their concepts concerning other forms of behavioral regulation such as social conventions (Damon, 1977; Turiel, 1983), game rules (Turiel, 1978b), prudence (Tisak and Turiel, 1984), and personal prerogative (Nucci, 1981). One central premise of that research is that children's social interactions in the context of a given domain (such as morality) are qualitatively different from the forms of social interactions within other domains (Turiel, 1978a). In this chapter, I will review the research that has attempted to identify the nature of social interactions in two domains: morality and social convention. These domains are distinguished from one another as follows (Turiel, 1983): Conventions (such as modes of dress or forms of address) are behavioral uniformities determined by the social system in which they are formed. While necessary for social coordination, they are not intrinsically prescriptive in that different forms of a given convention could achieve the same social organizational goal. Concepts about social convention are structured by underlying conceptions of the social system. In contrast with convention, moral considerations stem from factors intrinsic to actions—for example, consequences such as harm to others, violations of rights, and effects on the general welfare. Thus, moral issues are neither arbitrary nor determined by social regulation. Moral concepts are structured by underlying conceptualizations of justice and beneficence.

As stated earlier, it has been proposed that there are patterns of social interaction that correspond to the definitions of morality and convention just outlined, and that, from those interactions, children construct their moral and conventional knowledge systems (Turiel, 1983). Since both morality and convention define aspects of the child's social shoulds and oughts, one rich area of focus for the study of children's moral and conventional interactions has been on events entailing social transgressions. It is in the context of transgressions that the social give and take provides information regarding the status of social actions and the attendant responsibilities of the participants. Such interactions have been characterized as entailing a kind of social grammar in which children negotiate, test, employ, and clarify social norms (Much and Shweder, 1978). In other places, children's responses to one another's transgressions have been viewed as efforts to repair the social fabric (Sedlak and Walton, 1982) and to negotiate social responsibility (Walton, in press). From my perspective, the form of such interchanges differs by domain. Within the moral domain, interactions would be expected to focus on the intrinsic features of actions and on the objective obligations that the effects of such actions place on individuals. On the other hand, interactions in the context of conventional events would be expected to focus on the normative status of acts (such as attendant rules), their organizational function, and expectations that individuals conform to such conventions as members of the social group.

Studies of Moral and Conventional Interactions

A series of observational studies has been conducted of children's interactions in the context of naturally occurring transgressions. With minor differences among studies, the observational procedures entailed providing a descriptive narrative of the observed event and recording the sequence of actions and statements on a behavioral checklist. In two of the observational studies (Nucci and Nucci, 1982a, 1982b), the categories were divided into those that referred to responses directed at the transgressor and categories that referred to the transgressor's subsequent behaviors. In the remaining studies, behavioral categories referred only to responses to transgression. Some of these categories referred to reactions based on the nature of the act itself (such as injury or loss statement, unfair act statement, emotional reaction), while others referred to aspects of social organization (such as rule statement, disorder and deviation statement). The procedure in each study included providing copies of the narrative descriptions to judges at the completion of observations. The judges then classified events into moral or conventional on the basis of criteria derived from the definition of the two domains. Analyses were then conducted of the correspondence between observed behaviors and event domain. Judges' agreement in classifying events in each study was above 90 percent. Examples of events observed in these studies follow; these particular examples come from a study looking at children's interactions in unsupervised playground settings (Nucci and Nucci, 1982a). The first example is illustrative of conventional events, the second of moral events. In each vignette the transgression is italicized.

1. Social Convention (Event 2, playground 7, age 11-14): *Girl (1) is sucking on a piece of grass.* Girl (2) says to girl (3), "That's what she does, she sucks on weeds and spits them out." Girl (3) says, "Gross!" Girl (2) says, "That's disgusting!" Girl (1) then places the piece of grass down and ceases placing grass in her mouth.

2. Moral (Event 11, playground 7, age 7-10): *Two boys (1 and 2) are throwing sand at a smaller boy (3).* Boy (3) says, "Dammit—you got it in my eyes. It hurts like hell. Next time I'm gonna kick your heads in". Boy (1) says to boy (2), "Hey, did you hear that? Next time he's gonna kick our heads in." They both laugh and throw more sand in the face of boy (3). Boy (3) then spits at boy (1) and runs away.

Responses to Transgression. There are two components of each conflict situation to be analyzed: responses directed at the transgressor, and the transgressor's subsequent behaviors. Previously published accounts differentiating moral from conventional events have focused solely on the first component. In this section, I will review briefly findings regarding responses to transgressions reported in those studies before turning in the next section to a presentation of data regarding transgressors' replies.

In the study employing the youngest subjects (Smetana, in press), observations were made of interactions among toddlers attending daycare classrooms. Two age groups were observed, thirteen to twenty-seven months old ($M = 20.76$), and eighteen to forty months old ($M = 30.08$). Findings from this study indicated that social interactions in the context of moral and conventional transgressions differ qualitatively by the second year of life. Both the toddlers and their teachers initiated responses to moral transgressions. In both age groups, the child victims of moral transgression responded in ways that provided direct feedback to the transgressors about the effects of their actions. Included within the toddlers' responses were statements indicating the consequences of actions, such as the pain experienced or the loss incurred. Such verbal reactions were provided with greater frequency by the older children. In addition, the toddlers reacted to moral transgressions through attempts at physical retaliation and through emotional reactions such as crying. Finally, these young children occasionally sought out adults to address their grievances.

Adult responses to moral transgressions complemented those of the children and often followed them in temporal sequence. Their responses also focused on the consequences of the acts to the victim. Adults interceded by adjudicating rights in a moral dispute, by pointing out to the transgressor the effects of his or her action on the victim and, less often, by attempting to divert the victim's or transgressor's attention from the act.

Adults, but not children, in this study responded to violations of conventions. For example, when one three-year-old boy chose to wear a girl's pink bathing suit to go wading, his teachers responded to the act as a transgression, although the boy and his friends appeared to be oblivious to this breach of decorum (Smetana, in press, p. 13). This finding is not a surprising one in that conventional acts are not in themselves prescriptive. Thus, knowledge regarding such breaches would not come from experiences with the act itself, but rather from experience regarding the normative status of the act. For the daycare toddler, this experience comes in the form of adult commands to refrain from norm-violating behavior and, less frequently, statements pertaining to aspects of social organization such as rules and statements regarding the disorder or disruption that the act created.

Three studies (Much and Shweder, 1978; Nucci and Turiel, 1978; Nucci and others, 1983) have examined children's interactions in the context of moral and conventional transgressions at the preschool level. Children in these studies ranged from three to five years of age. In each study, as in Smetana's (in press) observations with toddlers, it was found that moral and conventional transgressions elicited qualitatively differing forms of response. As was found with toddlers, both children and adults in the preschool studies responded to moral transgressions. Preschool children, like toddlers, responded to moral breaches with statements of injury or loss, emotional reactions, attempts at retaliation, and by involving adults. As one would expect, these older children provided a greater proportion of explicit statements regarding the loss or injury experienced, and they provided fewer strictly emotional outbursts (such as crying) than was observed with toddlers. Despite their increased verbalization, the preschool children in these studies did not respond to moral transgressions in terms of the social order. That is, they did not invoke rules or social standards as the reasons for objecting to the acts.

Like the children, adults did not respond to moral transgressions through appeals to rules or normative expectations nearly as frequently as they provided such responses to breaches of convention. As in the toddler study, the adults observed in the preschools provided responses that complemented those of the children—that is, adult responses to moral transgressions focused on the effects of the act on the victim.

In one of the preschool studies (Nucci and Turiel, 1978), as in the toddler study, there were no observed child responses to breaches of convention. However, the other two studies (Much and Schweder, 1978; Nucci and others, 1983) did report child responses to conventional events. These latter studies distinguished between general conventions, such as gender-related clothing norms (for example, dresses for girls, not boys), and conventional school regulations (such as designated play areas). Both children and adults responded to violations of general conventions. Almost all responses to school regulations, however, came from adults. Children's responses to conventional breaches in the study conducted by Nucci and others (1983) focused on social rules ("Boys don't play with baby dolls!") and requests for adult intervention. Much and Shweder (1978) used a somewhat different procedure from that employed by Nucci and others (1983); they analyzed linguistic bouts rather than employing a behavioral checklist. Nonetheless, Much and Shweder also reported that children's discussions of conventional transgressions dealt with social expectations and norms.

Adult responses to convention in all three preschool studies, as in the toddler study, focused upon aspects of the social order. Relative to the responses provided to toddlers, teachers in the preschools provided considerably fewer simple commands and increased the rate at which they provided rule statements and responses indicating that acts were disruptive or created disorder.

The two remaining studies in this series have looked at interactions among older children. One of these (Nucci and Nucci, 1982b) focused on interactions in second-, fifth-, and seventh-grade classrooms, and in teacher-monitored school playground settings. The other (Nucci and Nucci, 1982a) focused on interactions in unsupervised parks and playgrounds among children in two age groups, seven to ten years and eleven to fourteen years. The pattern of interactions in both studies was consistent with what had been observed with younger children. In both the unsupervised play and school contexts, children's responses to moral transgressions focused on the intrinsic features of acts. One age-related shift in response type observed in school settings was a great reduction in attempts to involve adults in responding to moral transgressions once children reached the fourth grade and a corresponding increase in attempts by children to retaliate directly against the transgressor. For their part, the teachers reduced their own spontaneous involvement in moral events as children got older and were only minimally involved at the seventh-grade level. Adult involvement in moral transgressions, however, continued to focus on the harmful or unjust effects of the acts and on efforts to get transgressors to consider the feelings and perspective of the victims.

Adult responses to conventional transgressions engaged in by grade school children pretty much paralleled the pattern of teacher responses at the preschool level. Age-related changes were observed, however, in the pattern of children's responses to transgression. Included among these was an increase in the frequency with which children responded to transgressions of conventional school regulations between the second and fifth grades; this was sustained among the seventh graders, suggesting ngreater involvement by the older children in the norms of an adult-governed institution. Observation of same-age children in unsupervised playgrounds demonstrated that children of school age also respond to violations of conventions in the absence of adults. Many of the violations responded to (such as criteria for clique membership) were unique to the peer setting and thus not a part of the adult social system. They were, nonetheless, binding in the social order of the playground. The children's responses to conventional violations in both the school and playground focused on the social order. With age, however, there was a gradual decrease in the use of rule statements in both contexts and a corresponding increase in the use of ridicule (particularly among adolescent girls) to achieve conformity to conventional standards.

Transgressor Reactions. Findings from the six studies reviewed provide a consistent pattern indicating that children's responses to transgression differ by domain. In this section, I will complete the picture of children's interactions in the context of moral and conventional transgressions by presenting data from two studies (Nucci and Nucci, 1982a, 1982b) that included recordings of transgressors' subsequent behaviors for each observed event. Analyses of transgressor reactions in response to adult and child responses to transgression have been reported in one other study (Walton, in press). Unfortunately, that investigation did not distinguish between moral and conventional events and thus did not provide data germane to this discussion. Nevertheless, the behavioral categories employed in that observational study to record transgressor reactions correspond quite well with those used in the research reported here and, thus, serve as independent confirmation of the utility of those categories.

The categories used to classify transgressor behaviors in the Nucci and Nucci studies were as follows: *apology or restitution*, statement indicating regret at having committed the act, or an action taken to remediate the effects of the act; *appeal to intentions*, statement indicating that the actor had not intended to engage in wrongdoing or for the action to result in negative consequences; *claim prior wrong*, claim that the action was justly taken in reciprocity for a previous wrong committed by the recipient against the actor; *deny harm*, statement that the action had not resulted in any unjust or harmful consequence; *denial*, blanket denial that the act had been committed; *question rule*, statement that no rule governed the behavior or that the rule invoked did not apply; *claim ignorance of rule*, statement that the actor had no prior knowledge of the governing rule; *appeal to circumstances*, statement that the action was caused by circumstances beyond the actor's control; *deride respondent*, statements questioning the respondent's authority, sassing back, and so on; *noncompliance*, continued engagement in the wrongful behavior; *cease behavior*, cessation of wrongful behavior without employing any other form of response.

The overall percentages of types of reactions provided by transgressors to peers in playground settings (Nucci and Nucci, 1982a) are summarized in Table 1. Findings regarding peer interactions in schools (Nucci and Nucci, 1982b) are summarized in Table 2. In interpreting the data, we divided responses into two general categories, those that reflected attempts to remedy the breach and those that constituted noncompliant or defiant reactions (such as *deride respondent* or *noncompliance*).

Since only descriptive statistics are provided in these tables, conclusions we may draw from them should be seen as tentative. It would appear from the data in both tables, however, that transgressor reactions to peer responses to transgressions tended to be concordant with the domain of the events. Let us first consider transgressor remedies. Though simple cessation of misbehavior was the most frequent remedy provided by both moral and conventional transgressors, transgressor reactions in the context of moral transgressions were more likely to focus on the intrinsic effects of the acts than were transgressor reactions in the context of conventional violations. Transgressors attempted to apologize for their actions or engage in efforts to make amends for the effects of their behaviors more often in the context of moral than of conventional breaches. Efforts to account for their moral transgressions took the form of justifications that their actions were in retaliation for prior harms committed against them, or took the form of explanations that they had intended no harm by their actions, or that in their view no substantial harm or injustice resulted from their acts.

Table 1. Mean Percentages of Frequencies of Transgressor Reactions to Child Responses to Moral (M) and Social-Conventional (SC) Transgressions in Playgrounds

Subject Age	Apology or Restitution	Appeal to Intentions	Claim Prior Wrong	Deny Harm	Denial	Question Rule	Appeal to Circumstances	Deride Respondent	Noncompliance	Cease Behavior
7–10 years										
SC	2	0	0	0	14	20	4	9	31	20
M	10	33	6	8	4	0	1	12	24	31
11–14 years										
SC	3	0	0	0	7	25	7	20	25	13
M	13	6	9	6	9	0	2	12	20	24

Note: A total of 902 events were observed.
Source: Nucci and Nucci, 1982a.

Table 2. Mean Percentages of Frequencies of Transgressor Reactions to Child Responses to Moral (M) and Social-Conventional (SC) Transgressions in Schools

Grade Level		Apology or Restitution	Appeal to Intentions	Claim Prior Wrong	Deny Harm	Denial	Question Rule	Appeal to Circumstances	Deride Respondent	Noncompliance	Cease Behavior
2	SC	2	0	0	0	17	6	2	9	22	39
	M	13	2	11	4	7	0	5	11	18	24
5	SC	0	0	0	0	3	7	3	10	38	40
	M	16	3	9	2	5	0	0	11	12	43
7	SC	0	0	0	0	4	4	3	22	35	31
	M	12	4	10	1	1	0	2	4	17	48

Note: A total of 615 events with child respondents were observed.
Source: Nucci and Nucci, 1982b.

Transgressors did not attempt to justify their moral breaches by questioning the governing rules. Instead, such social-order responses tended to be given in reaction to accusations of breaches of convention. Such *question rule* reactions were provided more frequently in playgrounds than in school settings. This result may reflect the more fluid social system of the playground relative to that within the adult-governed social institution, the school.

In considering noncompliant reactions, we can identify two behavioral categories, *deride respondent* and *noncompliance*, which are indices of the willingness of transgressors to challenge or ignore the authority of peer respondents. There were no clear differences in the frequencies with which transgressors provided *deride respondent* behaviors as a function of setting, nor at the younger ages were there any clear differences in the tendencies for children to deride respondents as a function of event domain. At the oldest age levels, however, transgressors were more likely to provide such reactions to respondents of conventional breaches than to those of moral transgressions. Challenges to peer authority in the form of *noncompliance* behaviors were also more likely to be provided in the context of conventional than of moral events. This pattern was seen with children at each age level and in both contexts. This finding may indicate that children, including transgressors, treat naturally occurring moral transgressions as more serious than breaches of convention and, hence, are less likely to continue to engage in moral violations. This interpretation is consistent with findings from interview studies (Nucci, 1981; Smetana, 1980, 1981), indicating that children at all ages generally rate hypothetical moral transgressions as more serious than conventional transgressions. The observed finding regarding noncompliance behaviors might also reflect a pattern of more powerful sanctions leveled against breaches of morality than of convention. These studies, however, did not provide data relevant to that hypothesis.

Findings regarding transgressor reactions to teacher responses to transgression are summarized in Table 3. As can be seen in the table, the pattern of transgressor remedies provided to teacher responses to moral violations was similar to that which they provided to peer respondents. Transgressor reactions to teacher responses to moral transgression consisted of *cease behavior, apology or restitution, appeal to intentions, claim prior wrong,* and *deny harm* forms of behavior. In addition, transgressors tended more often to provide *denial* reactions to teacher responses to moral than to responses to conventional transgressions. No consistent pattern in the use of denial as a function of event domain was found in transgressor reaction to peers. The finding of a consistent pattern with teachers probably reflects the fact that teachers are responding to moral transgressions as third parties rather than as victims. Thus, the teacher respondents may be seen as less cognizant of what transpired and hence more likely to believe the denial than would a child victim. On the other hand, teachers respond

Table 3. Mean Percentages of Frequencies of Transgressor Reactions to Teacher Responses to Moral (M) and Social-Conventional (SC) Transgressions

Grade Level		Apology or Restitution	Appeal to Intentions	Claim Prior Wrong	Deny Harm	Denial	Question Rule	Claim Ignorance of Rule	Appeal to Circumstances	Deride Respondent	Non-compliance	Cease Behavior
2	SC	1	0	0	0	1	1	1	1	1	24	71
	M	8	3	13	5	15	0	0	5	2	13	36
5	SC	2	0	0	0	2	4	4	1	3	19	65
	M	6	6	24	2	12	2	0	2	8	9	26
7	SC	2	0	0	0	3	3	1	3	17	19	53
	M	7	2	20	5	24	0	0	0	2	5	34

Note: A total of 1,017 events with teacher respondents were observed.
Source: Nucci and Nucci, 1982b.

directly to child conventional violations and thus, in those situations, have the perspective of first-party participants.

Transgressor reactions to teacher response to conventional transgressions, though different from their behaviors in the context of moral events, are less differentiated than when reacting to peers. Nearly all transgressor behaviors in the context of conventions are accounted for by two categories: *cease behavior* and *noncompliance*. The extent of noncompliance is somewhat less with teachers than with peers, though the pattern of fewer noncompliant reactions to responses to moral than to responses to conventional transgressions is similar. The tendency to deride teachers as respondents is considerably less than was observed with peers, although there is a sharp upturn in *deride respondent* behaviors provided by seventh graders in reaction to teacher responses to breaches of convention. This finding may reflect the development at about twelve to thirteen years of age of Level 4 conceptions of convention as nothing but the dictates of authority (Turiel, 1983). In other research, Geiger and Turiel (1983) have reported a positive relationship between Level 4 negation of convention and defiance of authority (such as sassing back) among junior-hihg-age children.

Summary of Findings from Observational Studies. In summary, findings from the observation of transgressor reactions to responses to their transgressions both complete and complement the pattern of responses children and adults provide to moral and conventional transgressions. The pattern of behaviors that emerges from these studies as typifying peer social conflict in the context of moral transgressions is as follows:

The transgression (such as hitting and hurting, stealing, or damaging property) is followed by peer responses focusing on the intrinsic effects of the act (that is, statements of injury or loss, evaluations of actions as unfair or unjust, emotional reactions). In addition, peers tend to avenge the action or avert further actions through attempts at retaliation or, in the case of young children, by involving adults. Peer responses are, in turn, followed by transgressor reactions. For the most part, these reactions either attempt to repair social relations (a) through direct apology for the act, (b) by efforts at restitution, or (c) by simple cessation of the behavior; or they attempt to explain or excuse the act by (a) claiming that it was justifiable retribution for a prior harm, (b) claiming that no harm was intended, or (c) claiming that no substantial harm or injustice resulted from the act. Transgressor reactions in a number of cases also include derision of the respondent and/or continued engagement in the transgression. The last form of reaction, however, is more common in the context of conventional events.

In contrast with the pattern of interactions observed in moral events, peer social conflict in the context of breaches of social convention takes the following form: The transgression (such as engaging in counter sex-role behavior, violating dress norms, or using an improper form of greeting) is followed by peer responses focusing on the social order (that is, rule statements, evaluations of the act as odd or disruptive, or efforts to achieve conformity through ridicule). Such peer responses are then followed by transgressor reactions in which the child either complies wiwth the norm, or challenges the respondent by questioning the rule, by questioning the child's authority to invoke the rule ("Youu're not my mother") or by ignoring the respondent and continuing to engage in the behavior.

The observed patterns of child response to transgression were evident in nascent form among toddlers and in successively more differentiated forms among older children and adolescents. The pattern throughout each age group is one that is concordant with the theoretical distinction drawn between morality and convention (Turiel, 1983). At each age, then, there is evidence of coherent patterns of interactions within domains that differ qualitatively across domains. These patterns appear to be sustained across social contexts; that is, they were observed in adult-governed institutions (schools) as well as peer contexts (unsupervised playgrounds). In addition, there is some evidence to indicate that such patterns are present among children in other cultures. The Nucci and others (1983) study reported here was conducted in preschools in the Virgin Islands.

The coherence in social interactions also provides evidence for a correspondence between social experience and social judgment. Responses to actions reflected children's conceptions of the acts involved. The use of rule statements, judgments of disorder and deviation, harm, injustice, and so on were not provided randomly but were associated systematically with transgression type. The relationship between act domain and children's social concepts was demonstrated more explicitly in three of the observational studies (Nucci and Nucci, 1982b; Nucci and Turiel, 1978; Nucci and others, 1983). In those studies, child observers were interviewed about transgressions they had witnessed. Children were asked whether the act they had observed would have been right or wrong if there were no rule regarding the act. In each study, in over 80 percent of the cases, children stated that it would be all right to engage in the actions observed in conventional events if there were no rule. On the other hand, in over 80 percent of the cases, children stated that it would continue to be wrong to engage in the actions observed in moral events even if there were no governing rule. From these data we may conclude that children render judgments about (moral) actions having intrinsic effects upon people that are different from the judgments they make about (conventional) actions whose propriety is a function of the social system.

Conclusions and Directions for Future Research

Peer conflict resolution has been viewed as important for moral development since the publication of Piaget's (1932) *The Moral Judgment of the Child*. What we have seen in the results of the observational studies reported in this article is that the forms of peer conflict within the moral domain are qualitatively different from those associated with social conventions. Further, we have seen in these studies that adult-child interactions in the context of moral and conventional events, far from being disjointed from the structure of child-child interchanges, complement the forms of peer interactions within the two domains. Finally, we have seen evidence of correspondences between types of actions within the two domains and children's social concepts. This latter point is taken up in greater detail in other reviews (Nucci, 1982; Turiel and Smetana, 1984; Turiel, 1983). These findings pose some serious challenges to earlier models of children's moral and social development, and they provide new directions for future research on children's social development and social education (see Nucci, 1982).

The research that has been reviewed here should be seen as a beginning with respect to naturalistic studies of children's moral and social-conventional interactions. At present, there are a number of studies under way that are attempting to extend that research. I wish to close this chapter by reporting on some of those projects as examples of directions for new work in this field. Smetana's (in press) study with toddlers has gone a long way toward helping us to understand the origins of moral and conventional concepts. Two studies now under way should provide additional information regarding the origins of social knowledge. In one of those studies, Smetana is conducting observations of parent-toddler interactions in the home. Her study makes use of procedures developed to analyze mother-child interactions in early language acquisition as a way of capturing behavioral exchanges pertaining to social values.

The second study concerned with origins takes a different tack, and has a different focus. In this study, Elliot Turiel and Melanie Killen of the University of California at Berkeley are looking at how preschool children establish their norms for interaction in a novel situation. The procedure involves having groups of three preschool children come together in a room with toys and a table and chairs. They are asked simply to begin each session at the table and to remain together for a prescribed time period. These sessions are repeated at regular intervals during which the children are videotaped. During the last three sessions, the procedure is modified to see how the children adjust to minor perturbations in their group composition. These three sessions begin with only two of the children present and have the missing child reintroduced midway through the time period. Turiel and Killen hope to learn whether, over the course of sessions, regular patterns of interaction emerge among the children (such as seating patterns, social hierarchy, activity initiation and transition behaviors, distribution of resources, inclusion or exclusion of members in activities), and, if so, (a) how such common patterns are negotiated and maintained, and (b) whether the pattern of interactions differ by domain (moral or conventional) of the events involved.

The Turiel and Killen study is but one part of a larger project being conducted at Berkeley by Turiel and his associates. In other research, these investigators are extending the studies with school-age children reviewed in this article to provide a more comprehensive picture of the correspondences between action and social judgment. In all of the initial studies conducted in schools, with the exception of Much and Shweder (1978), observations within a given site totaled no more than four hours. While this procedure allowed researchers with limited resources to focus on multiple sites, it did not permit an analysis of how observed events fit in with the overall pattern of interactions that had preceded and perhaps precipitated the events that were observed. In the Turiel project now under way, repeated observations are being conducted within two elementary schools over a two-year period. This procedure should permit an analysis not only of individual events but also of how such events fit into the overall pattern of interactions within the classroom over time. In addition to conducting extensive observations, these investigators are conducting in-depth interviews of children regarding hypothetical moral and conventional events and regarding naturally occurring events they were involved in either as transgressors, victims, or witnesses. Through such interviews, the Berkeley group hopes to be able to determine how in actual situations the child's interpretation of events corresponds with the domain of the transgression, the child's actions in the event, and the child's future behavior in similar contexts.

While each of the ongoing projects just described deals with an important aspect of children's interactions leading to the development of their moral and conventional concepts, many questions will remain unanswered. It will be up to future studies and the work of additional investigators to complete the picture of children's interactions in the moral and conventional domains.

References

Aronfreed, J. *Conduct and Conscience: The Socialization of Internalized Control over Behavior.* New York: Academic Press, 1968.

Damon, W. *The Social World of the Child.* San Francisco: Jossey-Bass, 1977.

Durkheim, E. *Moral Education.* New York: Free Press, 1961.

Geiger, K., and Turiel, E. "Disruptive School Behavior and Concepts of Social Convention in Early Adolescence." *Journal of Educational Psychology,* 1983, 5, 677-685.

Hogan, R. "Moral Conduct and Moral Character: A Psychological Perspective." *Psychological Bulletin,* 1973, 79, 217-232.

Hook, J. G. "Development of Equity and Altruism in Judgments of Reward and Damage Allocation." *Developmental Psychology,* 1982, 18 (6), 825-834.

Kohlberg, L. *Essays on Moral Development—Volume 1: The Philosophy of Moral Development.* New York: Harper & Row, 1981.

Much, N., and Shweder, R. "Speaking of Rules: The Analysis of Culture in Breach." In W. Damon (Ed.), *Moral Development.* New Directions for Child Development, no. 2. San Francisco: Jossey-Bass, 1978.

Nucci, L. "The Development of Personal Concepts: A Domain Distinct from Moral or Societal Concepts." *Child Development*, 1981, *52* (1), 114-121.

Nucci, L. "Conceptual Development in the Moral and Conventional Domains: Implications for Values Education." *Review of Educational Research*, 1982, *52* (1), 93-122.

Nucci, L., and Nucci, M. S. "Children's Responses to Moral and Social-Conventional Transgressions in Free-Play Settings." *Child Development*, 1982a, *53* (5), 1337-1342.

Nucci, L., and Nucci, M. S. "Children's Social Interactions in the Context of Moral and Conventional Transgressions." *Child Development*, 1982b, *53* (2), 403-412.

Nucci, L., and Turiel, E. "Social Interactions and the Development of Social Concepts in Preschool Children." *Child Development*, 1978, *49* (1), 400-407.

Nucci, L., Turiel, E., and Encarnacion-Gawrych, G. "Children's Social Interactions and Social Concepts: Analyses of Morality and Convention in the Virgin Islands." *Journal of Cross-Cultural Psychology*, 1983, *14* (4), 469-487.

Piaget, J. *The Moral Judgment of the Child.* New York: Free Press, 1932.

Sedlak, A., and Walton, M. D. "Sequencing in Social Repair: A Markov Grammer of Children's Discourse About Transgressions." *Developmental Review*, 1982, *2* (2), 305-329.

Smetana, J. "Prosocial Events and Transgressions in the Moral and Societal Domains." Paper presented at the annual meeting of the American Educational Research Association, Boston, April 1980.

Smetana, J. "Preschool Children's Conceptions of Moral and Social Rules." *Child Development*, 1981, *52* (4), 1333-1336.

Smetana, J. "Toddlers' Social Interactions Regarding Moral and Conventional Transgressions." *Child Development*, in press.

Tisak, M., and Turiel, E. "Children's Conceptions of Moral and Prudential Rules." *Child Development*, 1984, *55* (3), 1030-1039.

Turiel, E. "The Development of Concepts of Social Structure: Social Convention." In J. Glick and A. Clarke-Stewart (Eds.), *The Development of Social Understanding*. New York: Gardner Press, 1978a.

Turiel, E. "Social Regulations and Domains of Social Concepts." In W. Damon (Ed.), *Social Cognition*. New Directions for Child Development, no. 1. San Francisco: Jossey-Bass, 1978b.

Turiel, E. *The Development of Social Knowledge: Morality and Convention.* Cambridge, England: Cambridge University Press, 1983.

Turiel, E., and Smetana, J. "Social Knowledge and Action: The Coordination of Domains." In W. M. Kurtines and J. L. Gewirtz (Eds.), *Morality, Moral Behavior, and Moral Development*. New York: Wiley, 1984.

Walton, M. D. "The Negotiation of Responsibility: Judgments of Blameworthiness in a Natural Setting." *Developmental Psychology*, in press.

Larry Nucci is an associate professor of education and an affiliate of the Department of Psychology at the University of Illinois at Chicago.

Peer discussion of moral disagreements can be analyzed to reveal processes of moral reasoning growth.

The Process of Moral Conflict Resolution and Moral Development

Marvin W. Berkowitz
John C. Gibbs

The concept of conflict in psychology traditionally has had negative connotations. Interpersonal conflict generally has been understood as antisocial and aggressive (Shantz, 1984). Psychic conflict typically has been viewed as an indicator of mental illness (Freud, [1910] 1977). Family or marital conflict has been viewed as signaling the breakdown of a social system (Lidz, Fleck, and Cornelison, 1965). The developmental perspective offers a much more positive view of conflict. Somewhat akin to weightlifters and bodybuilders who claim that there is "no gain without pain," many developmentalists argue that there is "no growth without conflict." This position is best elaborated by Piaget (1970) and his proponents. Indeed, the Piagetian concept of disequilibrium has been translated to mean "cognitive conflict" in the developmental literature. Under either name it refers to the experience of cognitive imbalance or tension due to the inability of the individual's present cognitive structure, or "meaning-making system," to make sense of a new experience or set of experiences. In the jargon of our current computer age, the experience "does not compute" according to our

M. W. Berkowitz (Ed.). *Peer Conflict and Psychological Growth.* New Directions for Child Development, no. 29. San Francisco: Jossey-Bass, September 1985.

present way of understanding the world. Hence we experience a state of tension or conflict. This conflict functions as the potential fuel or impetus for growth. Conflict therefore is viewed as a developmental stimulus, rather than as a psychological breakdown.

Developmental conflict, the rubric we apply to such phenomena, has been studied extensively both in the empirical cognitive literature and in applications to education. These studies typically rely either on (1) conflict derived from "surprising" aspects of the physical environment that violate the structurally generated expectations of the individual or on (2) socially induced conflict from the confrontations, usually in discussion, of differing points of view. While it is clear that such manipulations do lead to development (Berkowitz and others, 1980; Gibbs and others, 1984; Maitland and Goldman, 1974; Perret-Clermont, 1980), and that they often do so more effectively than alternative manipulations such as direct reinforcement (McCann and Prentice, 1981), there is still a great deal of controversy as to whether such conflict produces development via the mechanism of Piagetian equilibration (Kupfersmid and Wonderly, 1982). Regardless of how such conflict produces development, it is quite clear that it does so fairly consistently and effectively.

Our work has centered around the developmental role of conflict resolution in the domain of moral reasoning growth. We do not find that the phenomena we study are all limited to the domain of moral development, however. In describing our thinking in this chapter, we will attempt to identify those processes that we feel are common to the various domains of development. Nevertheless, our general framework derives from Kohlberg's (1984) theory of moral reasoning development.

Two central questions may be raised concerning developmental conflict resolution. The first question asks what forms of conflict resolution effectively lead to development. The second question asks how such processes develop. In this chapter we will treat both of these questions; however, we will focus predominantly on the second question. The first has already been fairly well documented elsewhere (Bell and others, this volume, Berkowitz, 1985; Lockwood, 1978).

The Conflictual Basis for Moral Development

The Kohlbergian approach to moral reasoning development essentially adopts the Piagetian concepts of stage and equilibration. The characteristics of a stage have been laid out most explicitly by Kohlberg (1984; Colby and others, 1983) and the nature of the equilibration process has been explored most extensively by Turiel (1972). It is generally assumed that development emerges from the discovered inadequacies of the present stage of moral reasoning as applied to specific moral problems that the individual faces. If the individual is ready for development—that is, if the current stage is sufficiently developed—and if the disequilibrium that results is significant enough, it is expected that the individual will construct the next highest stage of reasoning to (1) solve the currently problematic problem(s) and (2) alleviate the disequilibrium.

This process may result from internally recognized situations of structural inadequacy or from socially derived conflicts. The latter may be instances in which social interaction highlights the previously unnoticed flaws in one's approach to a problem or in which the positions of the two (or more) individuals confronting the same problem are incompatible but the solution to that incompatibility is not readily understandable. Due to the focus of this volume, we will limit our discussion to the socially induced processes of developmental conflict.

In the moral development literature, the typical mechanism for socially induced developmental conflict is peer discussion of moral problems. This technique, a derivation of Kohlberg's original stage assessment procedure, was first used as a developmental stimulant by Moshe Blatt in his dissertation and in follow-up studies (Blatt and Kohlberg, 1975). Subsequently, a substantial literature on moral discussion interventions was generated (see reviews by Berkowitz, 1981; Higgins, 1980; Lockwood, 1978). Based upon these studies we now can speak of two sets of moral discussion variables: person/context variables and discussion process variables.

The former set of variables includes the stage(s) of moral reasoning, experimenter/teacher instructions, stage match/mismatch, discussant relationship, degree of disagreement on problem solutions, and so on. All of these variables have been implicated in the developmental effectiveness of moral discussion interventions, and there is at least minimal empirical evidence to support each of them. For instance, Lockwood (1978) concludes that lower-stage subjects are more easily influenced, Maitland and Goldman (1974) have demonstrated the effects of experimenter instructions, and Berkowitz, Gibbs, and Broughton (1980) have reported the effect of dyadic stage mismatch. Furthermore, a number of plans for implementing developmental moral discussion in classroom situations have been presented (for example, Arbuthnot and Faust, 1981; Galbraith and Jones, 1976). Such educational applications, however, typically only inconsistently reflect the empirical literature on the effectiveness of moral discussion (see Berkowitz, 1981).

The second set of variables affecting the developmental effectiveness of moral conflict resolution focuses on the *process* of moral discussion. This has been a much less widely studied aspect of developmental conflict resolution. The earliest work in this direction was reported in the areas of Piagetian conservation (Miller and Brownell, 1975; Silverman and Geiringer, 1973) and categorization (Langer, 1969). These and more recent studies (such as Ames and Murray, 1982; Bearison, 1982; Russell, 1982) have demonstrated that such processes may indeed be identified and cannot be reduced to modeling or social compliance effects. The most detailed analyses of the process of developmental conflict resolution have been in the moral reasoning domain. Our own work on moral discussion analysis (Berkowitz and Gibbs, 1983) and related efforts by Damon and Killen (1982) and Powers (1982) represent a detailed description of the ways in which moral discussion can lead to development.

Berkowitz and Gibbs, (1983) have labeled the adolescent developmental process of moral conflict discussion a "transactive" discussion and have defined it centrally as reasoning about one's fellow discussants' reasoning. After having demonstrated that a series of five weekly moral dialogues can produce individual moral reasoning growth (Berkowitz and others, 1980), they analyzed the dialogues for forms of developmental process. The prevalence of the eighteen types of transactive discussion behavior (Berkowitz and Gibbs, 1979; see Figure 1) was positively related to the likelihood of resultant individual growth and predicted it more strongly than did the individuals' stages of moral reasoning or the match/mismatch between them. Damon and Killen (1982) adapted some of the transactive categories in their study of the moral conflict resolution process in children's interactions and found that such processes also were significantly related to ensuing individual growth in this younger age group. Powers's (1982) study of family interactions did not use a pre-post intervention design but did find that individuals' stages of moral reasoning were correlated with their degree of usage of transactive discussion in family moral conflict discussions.

Taranto (1984), in a more recent study, has examined the relationship between discussant stage mismatch and development from the perspective of developmental process. She has done so by employing a molecular analysis of actual utterances in moral dialogues; that is, she has examined the stage of each utterance and analyzed sequential patterns. In a reanalysis of the Berkowitz and Gibbs (1983) data, she has found that less than a full stage mismatch is related to an equivalent degree of change in the same direction as the mismatch for the lower-stage member of the dyad. Taranto directly relates this to the equilibration process. Hence we have evidence for the developmental impact of two conflict resolution processes: transactive discussion and microstage mismatch. In addition, Powers (1982) has reported evidence that suggests that supportive behavior by parents in family conflict resolutions may also be related to relatively advanced moral reasoning in adolescents.

This leads us to another level of process analysis. Research in education (Kohlberg, 1985; Power, 1985), the family (Lickona, 1983); Speicher-Dubin, 1982), corrections (Hickey and Scharf, 1980; Jennings and Kohlberg, 1983), and workplace democracy (Higgins and Gordon, 1985) has revealed that the general "atmosphere" of conflict resolution in such institutions is strongly related to the level of moral reasoning manifested by the members of those institutions. Let us use fairness in the family as

Figure 1. Table of Transacts

A. REPRESENTATIONAL TRANSACTS
1. *Feedback Request* (R): Do you understand or agree with my position?
2. *Paraphrase* (R):
   (a) I can understand and paraphrase your position or reasoning.
   (b) Is my paraphrase of your reasoning accurate?
3. *Justification Request* (R): Why do you say that?
4. *Juxtaposition* (R): Your position is X and my position is Y.
5. *Dyad Paraphrase* (R): Here is a paraphrase of a shared position.
6. *Competitive Juxtaposition* (R): I will make a concession to your position, but also reaffirm part of my position.

B. HYBRID TRANSACTS
7. *Completion* (R/O): I can complete or continue your unfinished reasoning.
8. *Competitive Paraphrase* (R/O) Here is a paraphrase of your reasoning that highlights its weakness.

C. OPERATIONAL TRANSACTS
9. *Clarification* (O):
   (a) No, what I am trying to say is the following.
   (b) Here is a clarification of my position to aid in your understanding.
10. *Competitive Clarification* (O): My position is not necessarily what you take it to be.
11. *Refinement (O)*:
    (a) I must refine my position or point as a concession to your position or point (subordinative mode).
    (b) I can elaborate or qualify my position to defend against your critique (superordinative mode).
12. *Extension* (O):
    (a) Here is a further thought or an elaboration offered in the spirit of your position.
    (b) Are you implying the following by your reasoning?
13. *Contradiction* (O): There is a logical inconsistency in your reasoning.
14. *Reasoning Critique* (O):
    (a) Your reasoning misses an important distinction, or involves a superfluous distinction.
    (b) Your position implicitly involves an assumption that is questionable ("premise attack").
    (c) Your reasoning does not necessarily lead to your conclusion/opinion, or your opinion has not been sufficiently justified.
    (d) Your reasoning applies equally well to the opposite opinion.
15. *Competitive Extension* (O):
    (a) Would you go to this implausible extreme with your reasoning?
    (b) Your reasoning can be extended to the following extreme, with which neither of us would agree.
16. *Counter Consideration* (O): Here is a thought or element that cannot be incorporated into your position.
17. *Common Ground/Integration* (O):
    (a) We can combine our positions into a common view.
    (b) Here is a general premise common to both of our positions.
18. *Comparative Critique* (O):
    (a) Your reasoning is less adequate than mine because it is incompatible with the important consideration here.

(b) Your position makes a distinction which is seen as superfluous in light of my position, or misses an important distinction which my position makes.
(c) I can analyze your example to show that it does not pose a challenge to my position.

Source: Berkowitz and Gibbs, 1983.

an example of this phenomenon. Under a variety of rubrics for almost twenty-five years, researchers have discovered that families in which conflict is resolved through fair and open discussion tend to produce children who reason at higher stages of moral thinking (Hoffman and Saltzstein, 1967; Parikh, 1980; Peck and Havighurst, 1960; Speicher-Dubin, 1982; Stanley, 1980). Lickona (1983) has expanded upon these findings to prescribe a formula for "raising good children" that relies heavily on a model of conflict resolution similar to those described above.

In summary, then, it is clear that the form of conflict resolution process is related to its developmental effectiveness. Included in the category of process are degree of transactivity, micromismatch of stages, open fair discussion, and social support. It is important to point out that the first two of these dimensions are not limited to the specific domain of moral of even the somewhat broader domain of sociocognitive development. As indicated by the literature on Piagetian domains cited above and by the chapters by Forman and Kraker and by Bell, Grossen, and Perret-Clermont in this volume, these processes apply to the logical (nonsocial) domains of cognitive-developmental growth as well. It is unclear whether fair discussion and social support are also applicable to nonsocial domains; further inquiry is necessary for such conclusions to be reached. This sourcebook should be considered in the context of the ongoing debate about the interrelationships of different cognitive stage domains both between social and nonsocial domains (Damon, 1981; Kegan, 1982) and within the social domain (Smetana, 1983). Whether one considers the domains to be independent, hierarchical, or simply correlated, it is clear that similar conflict resolution processes are related to individual growth in many logical and social-cognitive areas.

The Growth of Developmental Conflict Resolution Processes

Only very recently has the question been asked of how developmental conflict resolution processes themselves develop. The first systematic treatment of the growth of the developmental process was offered by Max Miller (1981). Miller analyzed the moral discussions of children in three age groups and presented a preliminary model of stages of moral conflict resolution, which he has recently updated (Miller, 1984).

We would like to spend most of the remainder of this chapter describing two recent investigations we have conducted that directly address the development of conflict resolution processes. Both of these investigations derive their impetus from the model of transactive moral discussion.

The first study (Gibbs and others, 1983) was designed to test the hypothesis that the Berkowitz and Gibbs model of transactive discussion was largely a model of adolescent logical forms of conflict resolution. To do this, twenty male and twenty female undergraduate dyads were formed so as to be homogeneously (1) nonformal operational, (2) transitional into formal operational, or (3) fully formal operational, according to Piaget's theory of adolescent formal operational thinking (Inhelder and Piaget, 1958) and measured by the Test of Logical Thinking (TOLT—Tobin and Capie, 1981). All dyads then engaged in a discussion of a moral problem for which it had previously been determined that they were in disagreement. The specific hypothesis was that only the dialogues of fully formal dyads would include any significant amount of transactive discussion, whereas the nonformal dyads would use no transactive discussion.

In order to test this hypothesis most powerfully, the eighteen categories of transactive discussion (Berkowitz and Gibbs, 1979) were critically reexamined. The original set contained what we termed higher-order (operational) and lower-order (representational) forms of transaction. Operational transaction is discussion in which one actively operates on (transforms) the reasoning of another. Representational reasoning is limited to *re*-presentations of another's reasoning without significant transformation. Berkowitz and Gibbs (1983) had suggested that only operational transactions were truly formally logical. Furthermore, two categories were actually hybrid categories that contained features of both types of behavior. Operational forms were considered to be more highly developed and had been shown to have greater developmental impact than representational forms. Therefore, for this study, we did not code nonoperational forms of transaction.

As depicted in Table 1, the results were strongly supportive of the hypothesis. Thirty-one of forty fully formal subjects evidenced one or more transacts in their moral conflict discussions whereas only eight of twenty-eight transitional subjects and one of twelve nonformal subjects did likewise. It is quite clear that transaction increases with the development of formal thinking. The data from the nonformals suggest an even stronger conclusion, however; that is, that formal operations may indeed be a necessary precondition for the development of the operational form of transactive conflict discussion skills.

Piaget (1972) has argued that:

Table 1. Transactivity by Level of Formal Operations

	Transactivity		
Operational Level	Present	Absent	Mean Percentage[a]
Formal	31	9	7.0
Transitional	8	20	1.9
Nonformal	1	11	.4

[a]Mean percentage of total statements that are transactive.

> The principal novelty of this period is the capacity to reason in terms of verbally stated hypotheses and no longer merely in terms of concrete objects and their manipulation. This is a decisive turning point because to reason hypothetically and to deduce the consequences that the hypotheses necessarily imply (independent of the intrinsic truth or falseness of the premises) is a formal reasoning process.... From the social point of view there is also an important conquest.... Hypothetical reasoning changes the nature of discussion: A fruitful and constructive discussion means that by using hypotheses we can adopt the point of view of the adversary (although not neccessarily believing it) and draw the logical consequences it implies (pp. 3-4).

It therefore seems reasonable to conclude that these data are consistent with the Piagetian model of development. Furthermore, given Selman's work on the relationship of interpersonal understanding to conflict resolution (Lyman and Selman, this volume), it is clear that cognitive structures are developmental bases for interpersonal competencies in conflict resolution. We still need, however, to explore the precise nature of the relationships between particular logical structures and developing conflict resolution capacities.

A second investigation that we wish to report is an ongoing one. Because the majority of the research concerning transactive discussion was focused on late adolescents and because much of the little work done with younger age groups employed adapted and selective versions of the transactive scheme, the question of how prevalent transactive forms of moral conflict resolution are in younger age groups was left largely open. Along with Fritz Oser, Marie-Madeleine Schildknecht, and Joyce Caldwell, the first author raised the question of the development of the original eighteen transactive categories (see Figure 1). Two parallel sets of data were collected, one in the United States by Caldwell and Berkowitz and the other in Switzerland by Oser and Schildknecht. In each country, two male and two female dyads were formed in each of the following age ranges: six to eight, nine to eleven, twelve to fourteen, fifteen to seventeen, eighteen to twenty. Dyads were formed to maximize opinion differences on one moral and one religious dilemma. Then each dyad engaged in an audiotaped discussion of the participants' responses to each of those dilemmas, according to directions from the experimenter to attempt to resolve their differences. In the following paragraphs, we will only report the discussions of the moral dilemma, although preliminary analyses suggest that the responses to the two dilemmas are nearly identical.

Given the small sample size within each culture and gender, we have decided to present the data summed across the groups. Table 2 presents the average percentages of total utterances that are operational transacts, representational transacts, and all transacts for each age group. As can be seen in Table 2, there is a steady increase of both types of transactive discussion with increasing age. The increase is much more marked for operational transaction than for representational transaction. Furthermore, the greatest increment in operational transaction is seen between the twelve-to-fourteen-year-old group and the fifteen-to-seventeen-year-old group. This is also approximately the time when formal operational thought is coalescing in the young adolescent. Nonetheless, contrary to the Gibbs and others (1983) findings, there is still evidence of significant transaction for some subjects in the nine-to-eleven-year-old group, when formal operations are assumedly at best nascent capacities. Analyses of discussions by the youngest group suggest their almost total lack of transactive discussion behavior.

These data clearly support the notion that the usage of transactive discussion is a gradually developing skill, perhaps with an appreciable surge in usage in early to mid adolescence. This raises another interesting question: If younger subjects benefit developmentally from peer moral discussion interventions, yet use only minimal operational transaction, then what discussion processes are generating their subsequent growth? A further analysis of the data is being conducted to ascertain possible

Table 2. Mean Percentages of Transacts by Age Group

Age Group	Percent Operational Transacts	Percent Representational Transacts	Percent Total Transacts
6-8	1.0	1.2	2.2
9-11	4.5	1.8	6.4
12-14	7.1	4.1	11.1
15-17	14.8	5.2	20.0
18-20	18.5	6.9	25.3

answers to this question. The data are being reanalyzed to look for forms of moral conflict resolution other than transaction that might typify the discussion of younger cohorts. These analyses are based partly upon the notion of representational transaction and partly upon the prior work of Miller (1981), 1984), Oser (1984), and Keller and Reuss (1985). All of these researchers have attempted to offer preliminary schemes for moral conflict resolution in children and adolescents younger than the subjects upon which Berkowitz and Gibbs (1979) transact model was based. It is hoped that the two sets of analyses of these data will generate an understanding of the developmental path of the processes of moral conflict resolution that have been shown to generate individual stage growth.

Conclusions

It is clear that peer conflict resolution is an effective means of promoting cognitive growth in children and adolescents. This is true both in logical-cognitive domains as well as in social-cognitive domains. As of yet, however, our knowledge of *how* such interactions promote development is merely fledgling. We do have a growing and substantial body of empirical findings that point to a variety of what we have termed person and context variables, most notably the absolute stages of the discussants, the relative disparity between their stages, the orienting instructions they receive, and their degree of perceived disagreement about the solutions (as opposed to rationales) to the problems being discussed.

A second, and more fundamental question has been studied much less extensively. That is the question of the interactional process of peer discussion effects on individual growth. We are beginning to focus on the forms that such interactions take by examining the actual interaction behaviors themselves. In doing so, we have come to recognize that certain forms of peer interaction are more effective in promoting individual cognitive growth. The bulk of this research concerns moral reasoning stages of development and is based upon the authors' work on modes of transactive discussion.

While we have begun to identify the modes of moral conflict discussion that promote moral stage growth, even less is known about the course of development of those interactional capacities. Two studies were presented here that begin to shed some light on this question. These data suggest that the developmentally richer and higher-order modes of transactive discussion may require the prior development of formal operational thinking capacities. Furthermore, it is clear that all forms of transactive discussion do gradually develop, at least from the ages of nine through twenty, with the greatest leap in development occurring around ages thirteen to fifteen and only for the higher-order operational forms of transaction.

Nonetheless, we still need to investigate more specifically the precise relationships between logical and sociomoral stages of cognitive development and developmental processes of peer conflict resolution. Are only logical skills necessary for such behavior to be available, or are social-cognitive skills such as perspective-taking also necessary? Are such prerequisites sufficient for the development of growth-producing peer conflict skills, or are some other processes also at play in their acquisition? Along with these questions, we need to pursue the cross sectional research on the development of transactive discussion presented here by studying other aspects of conflictual interaction in children and adolescents. Toward this end, some of the other strategies in this volume are eminently helpful, as is the ongoing second analysis of our cross-cultural cross-sectional data described above. With continuing research in these "new directions," we will understand better how children develop through conflict and therefore how to support, enhance, and remediate such growth.

References

Ames, G., and Murray, F. B. "When Two Wrongs Make a Right: Promoting Cognitive Change by Social Conflict."*Developmental Psychology*, 1982, *18* (6), 894-897.

Arbuthnot, J. B., and Faust, D. *Teaching Moral Reasoning: Theory and Practice.* New York: Harper & Row, 1981.

Bearison, D. J. "New Directions in Studies of Social Interaction and Cognitive Growth." In F. Serafica (Ed.), *Social Cognition, Context, and Social Behavior: A Developmental Perspective.* New York: Guilford, 1982.

Berkowitz, M. W. "A Critical Appraisal of the Educational and Psychological Perspectives on Moral Discussion." *Journal of Educational Thought*, 1981, 15 (1), 20-33.

Berkowitz, M. W. "The Role of Discussion in Moral Education." In M. W. Berkowitz and F. Oser (Eds.), *Moral Education: Theory and Application.* Hillsdale, N.J.: Lawrence Erlbaum, 1985.

Berkowitz, M. W., and Gibbs, J. C. *A Preliminary Manual for Coding Transactive Features of Dyadic Discussion.* Unpublished manuscript, Marquette University, 1979.

Berkowitz, M. W., and Gibbs, J. C. "Measuring the Developmental Features of Moral Discussion." *Merrill-Palmer Quarterly*, 1983, *29* (4), 399-410.

Berkowitz, M. W., Gibbs, J. C., and Broughton, J. M. "The Relation of Moral Judgment State Disparity to Developmental Effects of Peer Dialogues." *Merrill-Palmer Quarterly*, 1980, *26* (4), 341-357.

Blatt, M., and Kohlberg, L. "The Effects of Classroom Moral Discussion upon Children's Level of Moral Judgment." *Journal of Moral Education*, 1975, *4* (2), 129-161.

Colby, A., Kohlberg, L., Gibbs, J. C., and Lieberman, M. "A Longitudinal Study of Moral Judgment." *Monographs of the Society for Research in Child Development*, 1983, *48* (1-2, serial no. 200), 1-96.

Damon, W. "Exploring Children's Social Cognition on Two Fronts." In J. H. Flavell and L. Ross (Eds.), *Social Cognitive Development: Frontiers and Possible Futures.* New York: Cambridge University Press, 1981.

Damon, W., and Killen, M. "Peer Interaction and the Process of Change in Children's Moral Reasoning." *Merrill-Palmer Quarterly,* 1982, *28* (4), 347-367.
Freud, S. *Five Lectures on Psychoanalysis.*(J. Strachy, Trans.). New York: Norton, 1977. (Originally published 1910).
Galbraith, R. E., and Jones, T. M. *Moral Reasoning: A Teaching Handbook for Adapting Kohlberg to the Classroom.* St. Paul, Minn.: Greenhaven Press, 1976.
Gibbs, J. C., Arnold, K. O., Ahlborn, H. H., and Cheesman, F. L. "Facilitation of Sociomoral Reasoning in Delinquents." *Journal of Consulting and Clinical Psychology,* 1984, *52,* 37-45.
Gibbs, J. C., Schnell, S. V., Berkowitz, M. W., and Goldstein, D. S. *Relations Between Formal Operations and Logical Conflict Resolution.* Paper read at the meeting of the Society for Research in Child Development, Detroit, 1983.
Hickey, J. E., and Scharf, P. L. *Toward a Just Correctional System: Experiments in Implementing Democracy in Prisons.* San Francisco: Jossey-Bass, 1980.
Higgins, A. "Research and Measurement Issues in Moral Education Interventions." In R. L. Mosher (Ed.), *Moral Education: A First Generation of Research and Development.* New York: Praeger, 1980.
Higgins, A., and Gordon, F. "Work Climate and Sociomoral Development in Two Worker-Owned Companies." In M. W. Berkowitz and F. Oser (Eds.), *Moral Education: Theory and Application.* Hillsdale, N.J.: Lawrence Erlbaum, in press.
Hoffman, M. L., and Saltzstein, H. D. "Parent Discipline and the Child's Moral Development." *Journal of Personality and Social Psychology,* 1967, *5* (45), 57.
Inhelder, B., and Piaget, J. *The Growth of Logical Thinking from Childhood to Adolescence.* New York: Basic Books, 1958.
Jennings, W., and Kohlberg, L. "Effects of Just Community Programs on the Moral Development of Youthful Offenders." *Journal of Moral Education,* 1983, *2* (1), 13-50.
Kegan, R. G. *The Evolving Self: Problem and Process in Human Development.* Cambridge, Mass.: Harvard University Press, 1982.
Keller, M., and Reuss, S. "The Process of Moral Decision Making: Normative and Empirical Conditions of Participation in Moral Discourse." In M. W. Berkowitz and F. Oser (Eds.), *Moral Education: Theory and Application.* Hillsdale, N.J.: Lawrence Erlbaum, 1985.
Kohlberg, L. *Essays on Moral Development—Volume Two: The Psychology of Moral Development.* New York: Harper & Row, 1984.
Kohlberg, L. "The Just Community Approach to Moral Education in Theory and Practice."In M. W. Berkowitz and F. Oser (Eds.), *Moral Education: Theory and Application.* Hillsdale, N.J.: Lawrence Erlbaum, 1985.
Kupfersmid, J., and Wonderly, D. "Disequilibrium as a Hypothetical Construct in Kohlbergian Moral Development." *Child Study Journal,* 1982, *12,* 171-185.
Langer, J. "Disequilibrium as a Source of Development." In P. Mussen, J. Langer, and M. Covington (Eds.), *Trends and Issues in Developmental Psychology.* New York: Holt, Rinehart and Winston, 1969.
Lickona, T. *Raising Good Children: Helping Your Child Through the Stages of Moral Development.* New York: Bantam Books, 1983.
Lidz, T., Fleck, S., and Cornelison, A. *Schizophrenia and the Family.* New York: International Universities Press, 1965.
Lockwood, A. L. "The Effects of Values Clarification and Moral Development Curricula on School-Age Subjects: A Critical Review of Recent Research." *Review of Educational Research,* 1978, *48,* 325-364.
McCann, D. C., and Prentice, N. M. "Promoting Moral Judgment of Elementary School Children: The Influence of Direct Reinforcement and Cognitive Disequilibrium." Journal of Genetic Psychology81139, 27-34.

Maitland, K. A., and Goldman, J. R. "Moral Judgment as a Function of Peer Group Interaction." Journal of Personality and Social Psychology7430, 699-704.

Miller, M. "Cognition and Moral Argumentation: Five Developmental Levels." Paper presented to the Conference of Social Interaction and Social-Cognitive Development, Starnberg, West Germany, 1981.

Miller, M. "Discourse and Experience." Paper presented at the Second Ringberg Conference on Moral Judgment, Ringberg, Bavaria, West Germany, July 1984.

Miller, S. A., and Brownell, C. A. "Peers, Persuasion, and Piaget: Dyadic Interaction Between Conservers and Nonconservers." Child Development, 1975, 46 (4), 992-990.

Oser, F. "Cognitive Stages of Interaction in Moral Discourse." In W. Kurtines and J. Gewirtz (Eds.), Morality, Moral Behavior, and Moral Development. New York: Wiley, 1984.

Parikh, B. "Development of Moral Judgment and Its Relation to Family Environmental Factors in Indian and American Families." Child Development, 1980, 51 (4), 1030, 1039.

Peck, R. F., and Havighurst, R. J. The Pscyhology of Character Development. New York: Wiley, 1960.

Perret-Clermont, A.-N. Social Interaction and Cognitive Development in Children. New York: Academic Press, 1980.

Piaget, J. "Piaget's Theory." In P. M. Mussen (Ed.), Carmichael's Manual of Child Psychology. New York: Wiley, 1970.

Piaget, J. "Intellectual Evolution from Adolescence to Adulthood." Human Development, 1972, 15 (1), 1-12.

Power, C. "Democratic Moral Education in the Large Public High School." In M. W. Berkowitz and F. Oser (Eds.), Moral Education: Theory and Application. Hillsdale, N.J.: Lawrence Erlbaum, 1985.

Powers, S. I. "Family Interaction and Parental Moral Development as a Context for Adolescent Moral Development." Unpublished doctoral dissertation, Harvard University, 1982.

Russell, J. "Cognitive Conflict, Transmission, and Justification: Conservation Attainment Through Dyadic Interaction." The Journal of Genetic Psychology, 1982, 140, 283-297.

Shantz, C. U. "Conflicts and Conundrums in Child Development." Presidential address presented to the Division on Developmental Psychology, the American Psychological Association, Toronto, Canada, August 1984.

Silverman, I. W., and Geiringer, E. "Dyadic Interaction and Conservation Induction: A Test of Piaget's Equilibration Model." Child Development, 1973, 44 (4), 815-820.

Smetana, J. G. "Social-Cognitive Development: Domain Distinctions and Coornations." Developmental Review, 1983, 3, 131-147.

Speicher-Dubin, B. "Parent Moral Judgment, Child Moral Judgment, and Family Interaction: A Correlational Study." Unpublished doctoral dissertation, Harvard University, 1982.

Stanley, S. "The Family and Moral Education." In R. L. Mosher (Ed.), Moral Education: A First Generation of Research and Development. New York: Praeger, 1980.

Taranto, M. A. "Microprocesses in Moral Conflict Dialogues." Paper presented at the Symposium of the Jean Piaget Society, Philadelphia, June 1984.

Tobin, K. G., and Capie, W. "The Development and Validation of a Group Test of Logical Thinking." Educational and Psychological Measurement, 1981, 41 413-423.

Turiel, E. "Stage Transition in Moral Development." In R. M. Travers (Ed.), Second Handbook of Research on Teaching. Chicago: Rand McNally, 1972.

Marvin W. Berkowitz is an assistant professor of psychology at Marquette University. His research interests include sociomoral reasoning development, sociomoral discussion, and moral education.

John C. Gibbs is an associate professor of psychology at Ohio State University. His research interests include sociomoral reasoning development, sociomoral stage assessment, and sociomoral education with juvenile delinquents.

Clinical intervention (pair therapy) with a primary focus on interpersonal conflict is a rich context for the developmental study of psychological growth (or regression) in troubled children.

Peer Conflict in Pair Therapy: Clinical and Developmental Analyses

D. Russell Lyman
Robert L. Selman

This chapter investigates troubled children's approaches to peer conflict. Our aim is to outline a developmental paradigm for analyzing the youngsters' understanding of interpersonal conflict and their strategies for negotiating with peers and to demonstrate the theoretical and clinical application of this model. Here we use *pair therapy,* a clinical intervention that grew out of this approach, both as a method of utilizing peer conflict therapeutically and as a research laboratory for describing the development of interpersonal negotiation strategies in troubled children. Through pre- and posttreatment structured interviews and periodic observations of the treatment of a pair of severely troubled boys, we use conflict negotiation as a tool to diagnose social cognition and social conduct, and we attempt to characterize change in these realms over the course of treatment. Investigation of this issue leads us to hypotheses about the relationship between thought and action in the social relations of troubled children, and these hypotheses point to promising avenues for future research.

In pair therapy, two children with significant interpersonal and intrapsychic difficulties meet for weekly sessions with an adult who provides a forum for negotiation and assists the partners in reflecting on their ideas and strategies. Through repeated experience in negotiating their differing perspectives, the children are given the opportunity to develop new skills and insight. By examining the *way* they understand and utilize their perspective in peer interaction, we are able to refine both our theoretical approach and the treatment it is based upon.

Empirical Approach: Theoretical Foundations

Our study encompasses the following three analyses: (1) the hierarchically organized (developmental) diagnosis of the troubled child's cognitive and behavioral attempts at conflict resolution through various negotiation strategies; (2) the use of this diagnosis to describe progression and regression across the course of treatment; and (3) the characterization of specific types of thought/action relationships in troubled children's approaches to conflict and its resolution over time. A developmental diagnosis calls for the articulation of a unifying construct along which both understanding and action can be described as more or less mature in relation to one another. In our research, levels in the *coordination of social perspectives* serve this function. With a developmental understanding of diagnosis, we can chart the clinical course and define progress, as well as begin to differentiate among the patterns of social cognition and conduct in children with different types of pathology.

In the interpersonal negotiation strategy model (Selman, 1981; Selman and Demorest, 1984), Werner's (1948, 1957) orthogenetic principle is applied to the analysis of how the child's developing ability to coordinate social perspectives is used in moments of interpersonal disequilibrium in contexts of potential or actual conflict. Orthogenesis as defined by Werner is a general regulative principle whereby development proceeds from a state that is relatively global and undifferentiated to a state of differentiation and hierarchic integration. At each level of increasing differentiation in the hierarchy, previous levels are integrated as foundations for further growth in the developing organism's functioning. Thus, the orthogenetic principle enables us both to use a model that identifies the child's developing social competency and to explain regression to less adaptive performance levels.

Social perspective coordination is defined as the child's capacity to differentiate and integrate the self's and other's points of view through an understanding of the relation between a peer's and the self's thoughts, feelings, and wishes (Selman, 1980). Within this framework, the coordination of perspectives and its elaboration in thought (such as in concepts of friendships) and in conduct (such as in interpersonal strategies for the negotiation of conflict) moves ontogenetically from a form of undifferentiated egocentrism at the lowest level to increasing capacity for reflection on and an integrated coordination of perspectives, both within the self and between self and other (see Figure 1).

Figure 1. A Coordination of Social Perspectives Analysis of Developmental Levels of Interpersonal Understanding and Negotiation

Level	Estimated Range of Age of Time of Emergence	Core Social Perspective Coordination Level (Theoretical Construct) (Selman, 1980)	Interpersonal Understanding (Friendship as an example of; Reflective Interview) (Selman, 1980)	Verbalized Social Action Strategy (Hypothetical Interview) (Selman, 1981)	Interpersonal Negotiation Strategies (Observations) (Selman and Demorest, 1984)
0	3–6	Undifferentiated/ Egocentric	Momentary Physical Playmate	Physically Mediated Dominance or Submission	Impulsive Fight or Flight
1	5–9	Subjective/ Differentiated	One-Way Assistance	Verbally Mediated Control Hierarchy	Command or Obeyance
2	7–12	Reciprocal/ Self-Reflective	Fair-Weather Cooperation	Reciprocity Mediated Exchange	Influence or Accommodate
3	10–15	Mutual/Third Person	Mutual Sharing	Collaboratively Oriented Coordination	Collaborate

Method of Study

The Subjects. We present in this analysis one pair of severely troubled boys as a prototype of a way to analyze thought and action developmentally in a clinical context. These boys were selected from a sample of twelve children (six pairs), ages eight to thirteen, who participated in the project. All the subjects manifested a serious deficit in peer relations, often through excessive withdrawal or aggression. The children were matched for pairs on the criteria of age, compatibility, level of interpersonal skill, and the dynamics of their disturbances. The duo presented here, "Jack" and "Dan," are one of three pairs of boys, one pair of girls, and two mixed-sex pairs observed during the 1982–83 school year.

Jack was age ten years, ten months, and Dan age eleven years, eleven months, at the beginning (1981) of their two years of therapy together. They were functioning in the average range of intelligence; both were severely troubled children. Jack was hyperactive, aggressively conduct-disordered, and transiently psychotic. His single-parent mother had difficulty controlling him or meeting his needs. He was frequently assaultive and, at times self-destructive in school. Dan had appeared to be autistic early in life, using only echolalic speech and showing little interest in other people. His life in a single-parent home was characterized by symbiotic enmeshment. His behavior in school fluctuated among withdrawal, aggressiveness, and bizarre, often sexualized, clinging to adults. Dan was prone to infantile tantrums and needed a consistent system of rules and consequences to structure himself. Our analysis focuses on the second year of Jack's and Dan's pair therapy.

The Clinical Approach: Theoretical Foundations. Pair therapy is based on the premise that growth as a social being is facilitated by the direct experience of interpersonal interaction and conflict resolution (Sullivan, 1953). In the process of attempting conflict resolution, the child is confronted with the fact that there are differing perspectives and that negotiation is required for their successful coordination. For the troubled child, these negotiations require regulated and consistent exposure to peers within varying degrees of external structure. The therapist provides a safe forum for peer conflict and stimulates, oversees, and reflects on the children's clashes of will. The troubled partners are exposed to repeated interactions in which their differing perspectives are brought to bear on a solution, the resolution of which affects both of them. This approach varies, both with the type of problems presented by each member of the pair and with the developmental tasks associated with the members' ages. This model brings a new perspective to existing literature on peer-peer therapy (Bender, 1976; Birnbaum, 1975; Fuller, 1977a, 1977b; Mitchell, 1976).

Pair therapy is introduced to each child of the potential pair as a time to play together and have fun, as well as a time to learn the skills necessary for making and keeping friends. Each child agrees to enter the therapy for at least one school year with the same partner and therapist. When working with latency-aged children, the therapist provides a snack, a private room (equipped with a video camera for observation), and a variety of playthings, such as clay, drawing materials, puppets, toys, action figures, and games.

The therapist brings a "third-person" perspective to the negotiations of the pair, and the treatment also involves a "fourth-person" perspective, that of the observer, located in an observation room. Clinically, the observer provides the therapist with another view of the interaction, not only between the children but between the children and the therapist. From a research perspective, the observer videotapes the session for later data analysis and possible reviewing by the children.

The therapists' role can be characterized on three dimensions: (1) *stage setting,* (2) *structuring,* and (3) *facilitating reflection.* Stage setting involves the creation of specific opportunities for conflict in a conducive atmosphere. As structurer, the therapist mediates peer negotiations, provides incentives, and sets limits, with the goal that this role will become less and less necessary. The therapist encourages the children to reflect on their own and their partner's behavior, facilitates constructive peer feedback, and, through role modeling, suggestions, and theoretical questions, brainstorms with the pair around alternative strategies for conflict resolution.

The therapist sets the stage by creating an atmosphere of acceptance and safety in which the children are free to express themselves, share their fantasies, and try out new ways of dealing with conflicts. It is emphasized that no one is alone in having problems, that this is a time to experiment, and that the partners and therapist have made a commitment to a year of therapy together. To establish a climate of safety, the therapist outlines concrete boundaries to ensure that those involved be spared serious physical or psychological harm and that excessive damage to the milieu be avoided. The children are also enlisted in setting boundaries by being encouraged to debate about what rules they want for themselves. Having set the stage, the therapist challenges the children to negotiate how they will spend the hour and how they will share food, toys, and attention.

Structuring is an ongoing extension of stage setting and involves forms of maintaining limits and mediating that vary depending on the nature of the pair. The adult acts as mediator both verbally and through physical presence, with the goal that this role diminish. For aggressive children, the therapist helps establish a safe distance; for withdrawn youngsters, he or she provides a soothing impetus for coming closer together in interaction. As a verbal mediator, the therapist draws withdrawn children into the negotiation and helps to clarify their frequently personalized and idiosyncratic statements. The therapist consistently refines the focus for any pair, assisting the children in defining what it is they are negotiating and in articulating their points of view. He or she also shows persistence in not tolerating strategies for begging the question, by gently and nonjudgmentally pointing out incomplete resolutions and by raising the question of fairness when someone appears dissatisfied.

It is hoped that through these structuring techniques the partners will be given the opportunity and the motivation to experiment with new and more adaptive ways of negotiating conflicts. Ultimately the therapist's goal is to no longer be immediately necessary in this process, and hence, when the children feel secure enough, the therapist may "step to the wings," where he or she maintains a psychological presence by prompting and monitoring safety. Being asked (rather than told) to leave the stage can be an indication to the therapist that progress is being made. These requests often signal increased confidence and intimacy which the therapist allows to flourish until he or she is needed again. The therapist may step to the corner of the room or observe from behind the observation mirror, but, in any event, the therapist maintains a *psychological* presence. The children know that he or she will be there if their conflicts become dangerous.

Structuring enables the process of reflection to develop. When the children feel secure enough to look at their behavior, they are encouraged to do so both in an *in vivo*, ongoing way and in retrospective evaluation of past interactions. *In vivo* reflection relies on spontaneous adult and peer feedback, while reflection after the fact is often facilitated by the observer or the use of video recordings.

The therapist seeks to help the children assess the efficacy and fit of their conflict resolution strategies *in vivo*. As the therapeutic alliance develops, the adult provides direct feedback or asks rhetorical questions, at times pointing out maladaptive strategies by dramatic role enactment. Often the therapist makes use of the critical distance of a play metaphor—for example, by constructing hypothetical situations for discussion or using puppets to play out the conflict.

The adult stimulates peer feedback by seeking the children's opinions of one another's negotiations and makes their reflections safe by counseling them on how to communicate in a supportive and constructive way. Should the interchange become too vituperative, the therapist intervenes. If the feedback is hurtful or distorted, the therapist helps the children to reflect on their own feedback, to test its ties with reality, and to think about how it may have been heard by their partner. In later stages of treatment, the therapist works within the alliance to train the partners to counsel one another around what behaviors are most adaptive.

Each child reflects on his or her own behavior and often can see parallels to the partner's behavioral and internal struggles with his or her own. Indeed, we have observed some pairs in a phase of growing intimacy considering themselves as twins. As Sullivan (1953) noted, by seeing one another's behavioral problems in action and by sharing their troublesome thoughts and feelings, the children can learn by experience that they are not alone in being so troubled. This recognition can make the child more sensitive to other points of view in moments of disagreement.

Retrospective reflection involves engaging the pair in stepping back from their interactions to develop a yardstick for evaluting and understanding their behavior together. This can be both part of a routine wrap-up at the end of each session, as well as an intervention that the partners come to expect will occur whenever they have had struggles that have not been resolved or whose consequences have carried over from one hour to the next. The observer and video system add an important dimension to this process.

In the wrap-up, the session's negotiations are evaluated with the goal of developing a capacity for self-observation that can be of use to the children in future moments of disequilibrium. During spontaneous struggles, the pair is also asked to step outside the heat of battle and, from the position of observers, reflect on the adaptiveness of their behaviors. This often cannot be done immediately but rather in the session following a struggle, after the dust has settled. This is a primary reason that continuity through meetings regularly across the school year is critical to this form of treatment.

Video recordings of the partners at play are valuable because of their relatively undistorted perspective. This feedback tool must be used with careful forethought, however, followed with sessions that reinforce adaptive ways of dealing with interpersonal differences. Watching oneself on video is a highly charged springboard for reflective discussion of strategies for conflict resolution and their alternatives, but it may be intolerable or damaging for certain children. For example, several impulsive boys "acted out" in order to avoid observing undistorted recordings of their own destructive behavior. On the other hand, Dan, a "borderline" child, experienced watching a tantrum of screaming, rocking, and fist biting with joy, as though it were a re-experiencing of the gratification of infantile needs and impulses that the original regression had provided. Thus, in reviewing the video, the child's need for distance and defensive distortion should also be considered.

This brief synopsis of our methodology for the clinical use of peer conflict exemplifies our hypothesis that, in structured situations, repeated experience of negotiating and coordinating different perspectives can facilitate growth. We now turn to the use of pair therapy as a laboratory for the empirical description of social growth. This description leads us to speculate on how social cognition and conduct are related in specific developmental pathologies.

The Empirical Procedures. Before and after an academic calendar year of weekly hour-long pair therapy sessions, all of the children in our study were given structured interviews to determine their competence level in reflective understanding of friendship (a domain of reflective interpersonal understanding) and in the hypothetical formulation of strategies for negotiating conflict resolutions between friends (see Figure 1, columns 2 and 3). The interview measures were the Friend's Dilemma (Selman, 1980), which yields a level of Interpersonal Understanding (I.U.), and two hypothetical Action Strategy Dilemmas (H.A.S.), adapted from Abrahami, Selman, and Stone (1981), which provide an assessment of the level of the child's hypothetical strategies for the resolution of conflicts. All the children's actual negotiation strategies were observed at six points during the therapy year by trained observers according to a periodic counterbalanced observation schedule with a seventh observation at treatment end for routine follow-up (Figure 1, Column 4). Jack and Dan's pair also included an observation of the first session.

The observer, located behind a one-way mirror, operated a remote-controlled video camera and/or recorded process observations of the first fifteen minutes of a session. The therapy room was furnished like an ordinary playroom with couches, chairs, several low tables, and a television that could be used for outside viewing as well as video monitoring. The remote control camera was unobtrusively located near the ceiling in one corner opposite the large observation mirror. The sound-proof observation booth was equipped with a video monitor as well as an audio amplifier connected to two microphones in the therapy room. The children were aware they were being observed, knew the observer, and in the beginning of the year were encouraged to explore the observation system.

Interview Measures. The Friend's Dilemma interview (I.U.) presents a hypothetical situation in which there is a conflict of interest between friends and utilizes this dilemma as a springboard for questions that tap the child's level of reflective understanding of six friendship issues, of which conflict resolution is reported here. The children's level of social perspective coordination used in the understanding of the interpersonal conceptions inherent in the dilemma determines their I.U. level score.

The Action Strategy Dilemma (H.A.S.) elicits negotiation strategies for specific hypothetical situations. The following dilemma was used to assess hypothetical strategies for conflict resolution. "You and your friend each has a pocket Atari game. One got broken. You think it was his and somehow got switched with yours. He really disagrees and refuses to give it back. How would you deal with your friend?" If, for instance, the child responds, "Take it from him" (or other strategies of physical force), it is scored as level 0; "tell him to give it back" (or other commands) as level 1; "Offer to take turns" (or other forms of simple reciprocity) as level 2; and so on.

Observational Measure. Process narrations focused on identifying interpersonal disequilibrium in contexts for interpersonal negotiation (Selman and Demorest, 1984). Each interpersonal negotiation strategy

(I.N.S.) was first identified by having two scorers observe the videotape or transcripts and reach consensus on the contexts in which negotiations were occurring. In the present analysis, each agreed-upon strategy in a "context" was given a major and a minor score. The major score characterizes the predominant level of the strategy, and the minor score is added in parentheses if the strategy is considered to carry the secondary influence of a higher or lower level. Whatever aspect of the strategy has the strongest interpersonal effect is given a major score. If, for example, the child says, "Give me that," while in the process of grabbing a toy, the score 0 (1) would represent predominance of the grab (0) with the influence of the command (1). The minor score is given one-third the weight of the major score.

Agreement of raters scoring independently prior to consultation on contexts for scoring (for example, what behaviors were considered conflict negotiation strategies) was found to be 83 percent in a recent study using this procedure (Selman and Demorest, 1984). In the ongoing study described here, interrater reliability by independent raters on observation and interview measures in this study was 60 percent direct agreement on major/minor strategy level for I.U., 93 percent direct agreement on major/minor strategy level for H.A.S., 76 percent direct agreement on major/minor strategy level for negotiation strategies observed using videotape, and 69 percent direct agreement on major/minor strategy level for negotiations in narrative.

Results: The Developmental Diagnosis of Thought and Action in a Single Pair

Specific details on this study can be found in Lyman (in progress). In this section, where differences are observed, they are not based on statistical analyses. They are meant to be suggestive and to point to the way developmental measures can be used in a clinical or case study context. Thus, for instance, when we state that interpersonal understanding is at a higher level in the posttreatment assessment than in the pretreatment, we mean this in a clinical-comparative rather than in a statistical or probabilistic sense.

Data from our analysis of Jack and Dan are presented in Table 1 for the pre- and posttreatment interviews (I.U., H.A.S.) and for the first and last sessions of their pair therapy (I.N.S.). These scores are expressed in terms of the percent of total strategies scored at levels 0, 1, and 2. Clinical descriptions of the first and last sessions (including verbatim excerpts) are provided in Figure 2, as is a flow chart of the year-long therapy process.

Social-Cognitive Assessment. At the beginning of the year, interview results indicate that the majority of each boy's strategies are at level 1 in his reflective understanding (I.U.) and in his hypothetical approach to

Figure 2. Pair Therapy Process: Clinical and Developmental Analysis

	Initial Interview	SESSION 1	SESSION 4	SESSION 6	SESSION 10	SESSION 12	SESSION 14	SESSION 18	SESSION 28	Post-Interview
Observed Clinical Process		Ambivalence around intimacy in phone play. Jack blames Dan for "bad habits," he gave him in previous year; dominates and assaults. Dan flees, bites self. Adult stops session.	Talk of being twins. Fantasy play around control in "cops and robbers." Dan preoccupied with aggression. Jack asks for help in sharing.	Jack's birthday wish: "I wish I could live forever with my pal Dan and you Mr. L." Jack is controlling at his own birthday; Dan cries, rocks, bites self.	Jack is impulsive; Dan bizarre, animal-like. Dan wins a coin-flip for a toy, and Jack tantrums. Dan says, "I set him up—we shouldn't flip coins anymore."	Boys share a fantasy of a house on fire, sing a Chanukah song together. Jack acts out when Mr. L. points out he took more than his share of snack.	Jack willfully controlling, giving and taking away from Dan. Insists falsely that his grandfather died. Boys end spitting on each other.	Jack acts out sibling issues. While he regresses Dan acts more mature. Mr. L. interprets the sibling displacement.	Boys negotiate around how to spend their last session, and on *how* to negotiate. Dan's higher level thinking influences Jack. They end with a compromise.	
Percent Level 2 Strategies in Observed Sessions	Jack: 0 Dan: 0	0 0	37 0	13 21	35 33	42 47	7 33	5 48	42 73	38 40
Contextual Events Between Observed Sessions	Jack is arrested for stealing and crashing a truck. Dan tortures animals in camp.	Mr. L. sets firm limits, reduces session time, initiates reward of earning pair time back. Jack threatens murder, suicide at home.	Jack is suspended for hitting a teacher. Dan is bizarrely aggressive and sexual with adults. They ask Mr. L. for time alone in pair.	Boys concentrate on sports play, with Jack as leader; begin trading snacks. After losing coin-flip Jack tantrums, shoves metal in electric socket.	Dan's therapist is diagnosed with cancer. He becomes bizarre, self-absorbed, perverted, wants to kiss Jack on the lips. Jack is aggressive but controlled.	Boys channel aggression cooperatively through toys, begin to watch themselves on video. Dan enjoys watching his own tantrum on TV. Jack begins cooperative suggestions.	Dan talks psychotically about sex perversions, and Jack acts out, unable to tolerate it. Mr. L. reinforces rules. Boys reaffirm their friendship.	Sibling issues recede. Mr. L. announces he is leaving. Dan's therapist dies. Jack spends day consoling him. Fantasy play around scarce supplies. Trading, sharing, negotiation.		

Table 1. Pre- and Posttreatment Assessment: Reflective
Understanding (I.U.); Hypothetical Action Strategies (H.A.S.),
and Interpersonal Negotiation Strategies (I.N.S.)

	Time 1 (Pretest and Session 1)				Time 2 (Posttest and Session 28)			
	Strategies or Concepts	\multicolumn{3}{c}{Percent Level}	Strategies or Concepts	\multicolumn{3}{c}{Percent Level}
		0	1	2		0	1	2
Jack								
I.U.	3	0	100	0	6	16.5	16.5	67
H.A.S.	3	0	100	0	8	25	37.5	37.5
I.N.S.	18	37	63	0	51	0	60	40
Dan								
I.U.	5	0	80	20	8	0	25	75
H.A.S.	5	40	60	0	10	10	50	40
I.N.S.	17	35	65	0	49	0	24	76

conflict resolution (H.A.S.). The pattern of their responses across these two domains suggest, however, that the nature of their functioning is quite different. Jack's interpersonal understanding and his verbalized action strategies are both within the level 1 range; Dan, by contrast, shows more scatter across levels and greater differences between his reflective interpersonal understanding protocol, which shows some level 2 conceptions, and his hypothetical action strategies, 40 percent of which are coded at level 0. In our view, this discrepancy may be due to the nature of Dan's pathology, which we will discuss later. (Although the relation between these measures has not been standardized normatively, they are theoretically derived from the same heuristic model and hence in this preliminary study may be compared conceptually, if not empirically.)

Data from interviews at the end of the year suggest gains in level of understanding and/or verbalized action strategies for both boys. We see an increase in the number of alternatives they put forth as well as in the range of strategy levels.

Both partners' reflective interpersonal understanding appears to be at a higher level than their formulation of strategies, suggesting their conceptual awareness of friendship issues is somewhat more sophisticated than theier ability to plan negotiations around those issues. It should be noted that we make, albeit tenuously, an assumption that these interviews elicit to some degree the child's highest level of social-cognitive competence at each assessment period. Under this assumption, Dan appears to have undergone more of a growth spurt than Jack. He has, for the most part, dropped level 0 responses, and the increased consistency of his verbal responses suggests that he has consolidated his thinking at level 1 and is well into experimenting with level 2 ideas. The increase of Jack's level 2 responses in conjunction with the appearance of previously unobserved level 0 responses suggests that Jack's thinking is more disequilibrated.

Observed Clinical Course. A developmental diagnosis of observed interpersonal negotiation strategies now allows us to approach the question of how cognitive change may or may not be reflected in behavior, and vice versa. Periodic systematic observations of pair therapy enable an estimate of the trend of behavioral change and allow speculation on how this change may occur in different pairs. What follows are a clinical synopsis and developmental interpretation of Jack's and Dan's first and last sessions. A comparison of the two sessions suggests that the types of strategies the boys use are radically different:

Session I:

The boys begin playing with a cart, with Jack giving orders and Dan complying. While Mr. L. structures rules, Dan becomes absorbed in his own image in the mirror. Mr. L. asks, "Do you remember what you decided you're going to do today?"

Dan: Flip coins. Every time somebody wants something different, flip coins. *(Jack begins to make mock threats to Dan, until Mr. L. intervenes.)*
Jack: *(Backing off and yelling to Dan)* Go get the phones!
Dan: O.K. *(Finds two toy phones.)*
Jack: *(Speaking into a phone.)* Dan, you want to go to the ballgame?
Dan: Yeah!
Jack: Well, you can't!" *(Snickering, while Dan looks disappointed.)* Come on, Dan, come on! We'll go to the game. *(Dan joins him.)* Ah ha! You're a sucker! There are no tickets for you. *(Dan moves away, looking hurt.)* Do you want to be my roommate?
Dan: Yeah.
Jack: Well then, go get the phone.
(Dan ignores him, instead standing in front of the mirror and pretending to be a chicken, squawking and flapping in complete self-involvement.)
Jack: *(approaches, saying)* Gimme those gloves! *(Yanks them off Dan's hands.)*
Dan: I'm nervous *(Hides behind Mr. L.)*
Jack: Now you're going to get it! *(Dan cowers in the corner while Jack puts on the gloves. Jack chases him around the room at first pretending and then landing "mock" blows on Dan, who looks terrified. Mr. L. restrains Jack, who first pretends, then hits Dan again until Mr. L. makes him sit to "cool off." Jack continues to accuse and threaten and finally Jack backs Dan threateningly into a corner, where he hits Dan hard. Dan screams and runs away,*

biting his own hand with a wild expression on his face. Mr. L. restrains Jack, who kicks at Dan while he cowers. Mr. L. ends the session thirty minutes early.)

Session 28:

(While Jack cuts huge portions of "good-bye cake," Mr. L. mentions it is their last pair hour.)

Dan: *(Without apparent affect.)* I feel sad.
Mr. L.: I feel sad, too.
Jack: You can cry if you want, Dan.
(As the boys finish eating, Jack changes the TV channel.)
Dan: I don't want to see that.
Jack: I do. I like it.
Dan: Don't you like Popeye? *(Jack shakes his head, no.)* I want to see Bruno.
Jack: Bruno's not on this one. Flip a quarter.
Mr. L.: What do you think about flipping a quarter?
Jack: Good.
Dan: No, we have to *think* first.
Mr. L.: How do you think we can work it out?
Dan: *(to Jack)* Wait, you watch your . . . you watch this part of the time, and the rest of the time, I'll watch Popeye.
Jack: No! Flip a coin! *(They debate, Jack rocking excitedly while Dan leans forward.)*
Mr. L.: Jack, what happens when you flip a coin?
Dan: Sometimes I get upset.
Jack: I don't mind if he wins, I don't mind if he wins.
Dan: We get upset . . . Jack, I have the feeling that you might get upset if I win.
Jack: I won't. I promise.
Mr. L.: And you *(to Dan)* might get upset if *he* wins.
Dan: Wait a minute. 'Cause I remember one time that when we flipped a coin at Pairs and Jack said he wouldn't get upset. . . .
Jack: That was last year. . . . Flip a coin, flip a coin!
Dan: . . . And I remember one time down at the soda machine and he wanted Orange and I wanted Coke and I won and I got a Coke and he didn't win and he got upset.
Jack: Flip a coin! *(Raises voice.)* Look, I won't get upset, all right?
Dan: I'm going to be mad. . . . You know, couldn't we do a little bit of each what we want to do?
Jack: Flip a coin . . . Dan. If I win, I'll have a surprise for you, O.K.?
(After a stalemate, the boys decide to take turns, leaving it to chance to decide who gets their turn first. Jack wins and the boys play outside for the rest of the hour.)

Developmental Assessment of Behavior. In the first session, with the boys' interaction around the push cart, Dan's internalization of the coin flip, and the make-believe play with boxing gloves and toy phones, the boys exhibit level 1 type behaviors. Demonstrating a clear dominance hierarchy, Jack commands and Dan obeys. Their strategies later become level 0 when Jack's interactions lose their make-believe quality and he begins his unmediated assaults. In his terror, Dan loses his level 1 integration, and, as Jack begins his accusations and threats, Dan physically withdraws into autistic self-stimulation. At that point, the therapist must provide verbal and physical controls for both of them.

Table 1 summarizes the predominance of level 1 strategies followed by level 0 strategies that emerged as the boys regressed toward the session's end. This suggests that the pair has not achieved an integrated stability within level 1 type behavior, nor do they show any trace of level 2 type behavior. When subjected to stress, both have a tendency to regress to level 0 type behavior—Jack in his projecting, aggressive orientation and Dan in his submissive and fearful withdrawal.

In the last session, the dominance hierarchy is also evident, but we find a shift from the first session's pattern of command/obeyance and assault/flight. In their negotiations, the boys are now coordinating better the self's with the other's point of view, as well as showing an increased capacity to observe their own behavior. They continue to experiment with the coin flip, but their method of negotiating has a strong flavor of level 2 inquiry, barter, persuasion, and accommodation. Ultimately this leads to a level 2 compromise of taking turns.

Table 1 shows that in this session, 40 percent of Jack's negotiation strategies and 76 percent of Dan's are coded at level 2, with none at level 0. A similar increase of level 2 ideas and strategies is found in their posttreatment interviews. We also find, in quantitative analysis not presented here, that many of the strategies that the boys try out together in this session are those that they put into words in their posttreatment interviews. Their understanding, too, that there are alternative ways friends can disagree and negotiate their differing perspectives for compromise is shown clearly in their interaction.

Developmental Analysis of Clinical Course. The two synopses of behavior provided here suggest a developmental shift in peer negotiation skills. Given the inconsistency of troubled children's interactions, however, a one- or two-shot developmental picture of behavioral level may be misleading and certainly cannot give a flavor of the process of growth. The chart in Figure 2 is a way of characterizing how these troubled children negotiate interpersonal conflict over time. In this analysis, strategies (I.N.S.) are quantified in terms of the percent of level 2 strategies in relation to the total number of strategies employed by each child during the first fifteen minutes of each observed session and verbalized (H.A.S.) in their pre- and posttreatment interviews. This reflects the rationale that the growth of interpersonal skills can be characterized as an increase in range and frequency of relatively higher-level behaviors. Relevant events outside the observed sessions and clinical course in the twenty-session, eight-month treatment are also summarized in this figure.

This picture of the clinical course suggests how behaviors that have many complex determinants, including external contextual events, the phase of the peer relationship, and cognitive competency, may yield consistent patterns over time. Clearly, accurate diagnosis needs to utilize data collected over time rather than at one instant. Despite the general upward trend, variation across the year is also evident. We speculate that this variation is typical of children with this significant a degree of pathology. Moreover, we can speculate that the pattern of fluctuations in the maturity of Jack's and Dan's negotiations is disequilibrium necessary for growth. By this we mean that flux involving a juggling of "old" and "new" ways of thinking and acting may precede the consolidation of a higher level of cognition and conduct.

Competency and Conduct: Implications for a Developmental Model of the Diagnostic and Therapeutic Use of Peer Conflict

This chapter provides a sketch of our program of research. It also suggests a number of characteristics that differentiate troubled children from their peers in the area of interpersonal conflict. On the average, the "generic" troubled child's interpersonal understanding and verbal strategies are delayed in relation to the ordinary child (Gurucharri and others, 1984). In addition, the troubled child's social thinking and behavior are more subject to regression, particularly when frustration occurs in conflict resolution (Selman and Jaquette, 1978). Our comparison of Jack and Dan suggests, moreover, that it may be useful to think of different types of pathology that have specific implications for treatment goals. By examining relationships between the developmental levels of reflective cognition (I.U., H.A.S.) and actual conduct (I.N.S), we suggest in the subsections that follow, three problematic approaches that troubled children bring to conflict resolution.

Undifferentiated Delay in Cognitive Competency and Interpersonal Conduct. The first type shows pervasive delays in which levels of cognition and conduct are both low and undifferentiated in relation to one another. The profile of their negotiation strategies over time is relatively flat, many of their interactive problems involve communicative difficulties, and these deficits inhibit their ability to articulate their ideas in interviews. Children with their pervasive pattern of deficits have limited ability to benefit from interpersonal disequilibrium. The major focus of treatment, therefore, might be direct training in social-cognitive skills, which can be practiced repeatedly in the peer dyad.

Unintegrated in Competency and Conduct. Jack exemplifies a second type, in which level of social-cognitive competency is not consistently reflected in level of conduct. Like many conduct-disordered children, Jack's problem is one of maintaining a stable integration of level of social cognition and behavior. Analysis of Jack's clinical course shows that he is capable of higher-level behaviors but that overall he tends to regress easily with contextual stresses. For children like Jack, the goal is to use interpersonal disequilibrium for cognitive restructuring and as a forum for helping them to identify and cope with those stresses that cause them to regress. Jack is also most likely to change dramatically if his context, in this case a chaotic family situation, is also treated.

Pervasively Unintegrated in Functional Areas of Self. Dan exemplifies a more subtle but also more severe problem in integration. Quantitative analysis suggests that he has benefited, both cognitively and behaviorally, from dealing with conflict in the context of therapy. Note, however, his bizarre ideation around sex and violence, and how syntonic and deeply gratifying regression to infantile states is to him. He likes to watch his own wailing, rocking, and self-mutilation on video.

Dan also does not seem to know if he really has feelings or what to do with them. For example, in the last session, he says, "I feel sad.... Shall I cry?" Dan's problem is not so much the lack of integration of social-cognitive and social-behavioral levels as the lack of integration of cognitive and affective aspects within the *self*. This is typical of borderline and schizophrenic children. His sense of himself is very unstable, and, although on the surface his strategies appear to be at a relatively high level, there are strong indications that they are not because they involve a disassociation of the affective and cognitive components of action. In other words, when Dan says "I feel sad—shall I cry?" it suggests that he experiences a situation that he knows in theory might make someone sad, but he does not have a way to make a connection between the experience and the affect. He does not really feel sad, but he is not simply pretending to be sad either. He is puzzled over the fact that that which he expects to feel or is told to expect to feel, he does not. Hence, the affective and cognitive components of his negotiation strategies are dissociated. There is a weak "self" that cannot pull the two together in any way that is real for him, so his ideas and strategies are often unintegrated imitations. Thus, it is in the dissociation across development of affective, cognitive, and conative components of interpersonal relations that we see a "borderline" self, an ego that cannot integrate the various component parts as higher levels of development and bind them to one another in a meaningful way. While Dan can clearly make use of pair therapy, his prognosis for the integration of high levels of cognition and conduct is guarded.

Conclusion

We have provided a speculative outcome of one approach to the therapeutic and diagnostic use of peer conflict in the treatment of troubled children. We present pair therapy and this developmental paradigm of interpersonal understanding and negotiation strategies as an approach to the study of issues around cognitive and behavioral change raised in this chapter. It is a perspective designed to open avenues both for future treatment and for research into the developmental diagnosis of thought and action.

In so doing, we must stress that the research undertaken in this clinical context and described here briefly is based upon two age-old procedural rules of empiricism. First, energy is directed toward making the constructs under examination both operational and reliably identifiable. Second, the collection and classification of instances of these cognitive and behavioral constructs are based on a relatively systematic and objective process of data collection, rather than on random or subjectively selected clinical impressions. In addition, through this approach the clinical process and external contextual events are also considered in an attempt both to construct a developmental model applicable to pathology and to develop a clinical practice that informs and is informed by research.

References

Abrahami, A., Selman, R. L., and Stone, C. "A Developmental Assessment of Children's Verbal Strategies for Social Action Resolution." *Journal of Applied Developmental Psychology*, 1981, 2, 145-163.

Bender, B. "Duo-Therapy: A Method of Casework Treatment of Children." *Child Welfare*, 1976, 55, 95-108.

Birnbaum, M. "Peer-Pair Psychotherapy: A New Approach to Withdrawn Children." *Journal of Clinical Child Psychology*, 1975, 4, 13-16.

Fuller, J. S. "Duo-Therapy: A Potential Treatment of Choice for Latency Children." *Journal of American Academy of Child Psychiatry*, 1977a, 26, 469-477.

Fuller, J. S. "Duo-Therapy Case Studies: Process and Techniques." *Social Casework*, Feb. 1977b, pp. 84-91.

Gurucharri, C., Phelps, E., and Selman, R. L. "The Development of Interpersonal Understanding: A Longitudinal-Comparative Study of Normal and Disturbed Youths." *Journal of Clinical and Consulting Psychology*, 1984, 52, 26-36.

Lyman, D. R. *A Developmental Study of Thought and Action in Pair Therapy.* Unpublished dissertation, Boston University, 1985.

Mitchell, C. A. "Duo-Therapy: An Innovative Approach to the Treatment of Children." *Smith College Studies in Social Work*, June 1976, pp. 236-247.

Selman, R. L. *The Growth of Interpersonal Understanding.* New York: Academic Press, 1980.

Selman, R. L. "The Development of Interpersonal Competence: The Role of Understanding in Conduct." *Developmental Review*, 1981, 1, 401-422.

Selman, R. L., and Demorest, A. P. "Observing Troubled Children's Interpersonal

Negotiation Strategies: Implications of and for a Developmental Model." *Child Development,* 1984, *55,* 288-304.

Selman, R. L., and Jaquette, D. "Stability and Oscillation in Interpersonal Awareness: A Clinical-Developmental Analysis." In C. B. Keasy (Ed.), *XXV Nebraska Symposium on Motivation.* Lincoln: University of Nebraska Press, 1978.

Sullivan, H. S. *The Interpersonal Theory of Psychiatry.* New York: Norton, 1953.

Werner, H. *Comparative Psychology of Mental Development.* Chicago: Follett, 1948.

Werner, H. "The Concept of Development from a Comparative and Organismic Point of View." In D. Harris (Ed.), *The Concept of Development.* Minneapolis: University of Minnesota Press, 1957.

D. Russell Lyman is a clinical psychologist, practicing at the Brookline (Massachusetts) Community Mental Health Center.

Robert L. Selman is director of the Manville School in the Judge Baker Guidance Center in Boston and associate professor of psychology in the Psychiatry Department of the Harvard University Medical School.

Index

A

Abrahami, A., 92, 101
Adolescents: collaborative problem solving by, 29-36; moral and conventional interactions of, 57, 59-67; moral development of, 74, 79; in pair therapy, 87-100
Aggression, physical and verbal as distinct, 12-13, 17
Ahlborn, H. H., 82
Ames, G. J., 43, 53, 73, 81
Anderson, C. J., 23n, 39
Arbuthnot, J. B., 73, 81
Arnold, K. O., 82
Aronfreed, J., 55, 69
Asher, S. T., 19, 21

B

Baldwin, J. M., 23
Bales, R. F., 16, 20
Bearison, D. J., 27, 28, 38, 73, 81
Bell, N., 1, 27, 41-54, 72, 76
Bender, B., 88, 101
Berkowitz, M. W., 1-2, 4, 20, 71-84
Birnbaum, M., 88, 101
Blatt, M., 73, 81
Bovet, M., 53
Broughton, J. M., 73, 81
Brownell, C. A., 73, 83
Budwig, N. A., 39

C

Caldwell, J., 78
California at Berkeley, University of, origins of social knowledge research at, 68-69
Capie, W., 77, 83
Carugati, F., 43, 53
Cazden, C. B., 28, 29, 37, 38
Centration, concept of, 44
Cheesman, F. L., 82
Children: as toddlers, 58, 68; at three years, 58-59, 68, 87; at four years, 43-53, 58-59, 68, 87; at five years, 43-53, 58-59, 68, 87; at six years, 5-20, 43-53, 79, 87; at seven years, 5-20, 43-53, 57, 59-67, 79, 87; at eight years, 57, 61-66, 79, 87; at nine years, 57, 61-66, 79, 87; at ten years, 57, 61-66, 79, 87; at eleven years, 57, 59-67, 79, 87; at twelve years, 57, 61-66, 79, 87, 88-100; in adolescence, 29-36, 57, 59-67, 74, 79, 87, 88-100
Clements, M. A., 30, 38
Cognition, bottom-up or top-down approach to, 37. *See also* Social cognition; Sociocognitive conflict
Colby, A., 72, 81
Conflict: background on, 3-5; behavior coding of, 6; concepts of, 3-4, 41, 7-1-72; conclusions on, 18-20; defined, 4; and disequilibrium, 24, 71, 72-73, 74; goals of, 18-19; issues of, 9-12, 15-18; and moral and conventional concepts, 55-70; and pair therapy, 85-102; rate of, 13, 18; and rule conceptions, 16-17; social-cognitive and sociometric correlates of, 3-21; sociocognitive, 41-54; sources of, 42; success in winning, 13, 16; tactics used during, 12-13, 17-18
Conflict resolution: growth of processes for, 76-80; and moral development, 71-84
Conventional concepts. *See* Moral and conventional concepts
Cornelison, A., 71, 82
Cunningham, E., 3n

D

Damon, W., 4, 8, 20, 56, 69, 74, 76, 81-82
Danaher, D., 20
Dawe, H. C., 4, 20
Demorest, A. P., 20, 21, 86, 87, 92, 93, 101-102
De Paolis, P., 53
Discovery, process of, 34-35
Dodge, K. A., 5, 18, 20

Doise, W., 26–27, 29, 38, 39, 43, 44, 46, 47, 53–54
Durkheim, E., 55, 69

E

Emler, W., 27, 38
Emmerich, W., 15, 20
Encarnacion-Gawrych, G., 70
Erikson, E., 3

F

Faust, D., 73, 81
Finck, D. N., 15, 20
Fleck, S., 71, 82
Fonds National de la Recherche Scientifique, 41n
Forbes, D., 19, 20
Forman, E. A., 1, 23–39, 76
Freud, S., 3, 41, 71, 82
Fuller, J. S., 88, 101

G

Galbraith, R. E., 73, 82
Geiger, K., 66, 69
Geiringer, E., 73, 83
Gender differences: and social cognition, 12, 16, 17, 18, 19; in sociocognitive conflict, 48, 51
Genevan research group, and social origins of logic, 27, 29
Gibbs, J. C., 1, 4, 20, 71–84
Giroud, J., 53
Glachan, M., 27, 38, 43, 53
Goldman, J. R., 72, 73, 83
Goldstein, D. S., 82
Gordon, F., 74, 82
Grossen, M., 1, 41–54, 76
Gurucharri, C., 99, 101

H

Hanson, N. R., 34–35, 38
Havighurst, R. J., 76, 83
Hickey, J. E., 74, 82
Higgins, A., 73, 74, 82
Hoffman, M. L., 76, 82
Hogan, R., 55, 69
Hook, J. G., 55, 69

I

Inhelder, B., 41, 53, 54, 77, 82
Intelligence, functions of, 24

J

Jaquette, D., 99, 102
Jennings, K. D., 15, 20
Jennings, W., 74, 82
Jones, D., 3n
Jones, T. M., 73, 82

K

Kegan, R. G., 76, 82
Keller, M., 80, 82
Kepler, J., 34
Killen, M., 4, 20, 68, 74, 82
Kohlberg, L., 55, 69, 72, 73, 74, 81, 82
Kraker, M. J., 1, 23–39, 76
Krasnor, L. R., 4, 16, 19, 20
Kuhn, D., 28, 30, 37, 39, 46, 53
Kupfersmid, J., 72, 82

L

Landau, M., 23n
Langer, J., 73, 82
Lesh, R., 23n
Levy, M., 43, 44, 53
Lickona, T., 74, 76, 82
Lidz, T., 71, 82
Lieberman, M., 81
Light, P., 27, 38, 43, 53
Lockwood, A. L., 72, 73, 82
Logic, social origins of: analysis of, 23–39; background on, 23–26; experimental and observational studies of, 27–29; peer collaboration study of, 29–36; and peer interaction, 24–25, 27; previous research on, 26–29; research needed on, 36–38
Lyman, D. R., 1, 78, 85–102

M

McCann, D. C., 72, 82
Mackie, D., 27, 29, 38, 43, 53
McLane, J. B., 39
McNamee, G. D., 39
Maitland, K. A., 72, 73, 83

Mead, G. H., 23, 39
Microgenetic analysis, 25-26
Miller, M., 76-77, 80, 83
Miller, P. M., 20
Miller, S. A., 73, 83
Mitchell, C. A., 88, 101
Monash Space Visualization Test, 30
Moral and conventional concepts: analysis of development of, 55-70; background on, 55-57; and classification of transgressor behaviors, 61-66; domains distinguished for, 56-57; findings on, summarized, 66-67; future research on, 67-69; studies of interactions in, 57-67; transgression of, responses to, 57-60; and transgressor reactions, 60-66
Moral development: analysis of moral conflict resolution for, 71-84; background on, 71-72; conclusions on, 80-81; conflictual basis for, 72-76; and growth of conflict resolution processes, 76-80; person/context and discussion process variables in, 73-74; transactive discussions for, 74-80
Much, N. C., 5, 20, 56, 58, 59, 69
Mugny, G., 27, 29, 38, 39, 43, 44, 45, 46, 47, 53-54
Murray, F. B., 43, 53, 73, 81

N

Nakamura, D. Y., 15, 20
National Institute of Mental Health, 23n
National Science Foundation, 3n
Nucci, L., 1, 55-70
Nucci, M. S., 57, 59-60, 61, 62n, 63n, 65n, 67, 70

O

Orthogenesis, and pair therapy, 86
Oser, F., 78, 80, 83
Overton, W. F., 28, 39

P

Pair therapy: analysis of, 85-102; background on, 85-86; behavior assessment in, 98; clinical approach to, 88-91; clinical course of, 96-97; competency and conduct in, 99-100; conclusion on, 101; developmental analysis of, 98-99; empirical procedures in, 91-92; findings on, 89-99; implications of, 99-100; interview measures in, 92; observational measures in, 92-93; and social-cognitive assessment, 93-96; study method for, 88-93; subjects in, 88; theoretical foundations for, 86-87; therapist role in, 89-91
Parikh, B., 76, 83
Parsons, T., 16, 20
Peck, R. F., 76, 83
Peers: collaboration by, 29-36; conflict among, 9-15; and logic's social origins, 23-39; moral and conventional concepts of, 55-70; moral discussions by, 73-81; pair therapy for, 85-102; and social cognition, 3-21; and sociocognitive conflict, 41-54
Peery, J. C., 9, 21
Peevers, B. H., 7, 20, 21
Pepper, S. C., 28, 39
Perret-Clermont, A.-N., 1, 27, 28, 38, 39, 41-54, 72, 76, 83
Phelps, E., 30, 37, 39, 101
Piaget, J., 3, 19, 23-25, 26, 27, 28, 36, 39, 41, 43, 44, 46, 48, 49, 52, 54, 55, 67, 70, 71, 72, 73, 76, 77, 78, 82, 83
Power, C., 74, 83
Powers, S. I., 74, 83
Prentice, N. M., 72, 82

R

Reese, H. W., 28, 39
Renshaw, P. D., 19, 21
Restum, M., 3n
Reuss, S., 80, 82
Rommetveit, R., 49, 54
Rubin, K. H., 4, 5, 16, 19, 20, 21
Russell, J., 73, 83

S

Saltzstein, H. D., 76, 82
Scharf, P. L., 74, 82
Schildknecht, M.-M., 78
Schnell, S. V., 82
Schubauer-Leoni, M. L., 43, 45, 47, 48, 51, 54
Scinto, L., 23n

Secord, P. F., 7, 20, 21
Sedlak, A., 56, 70
Selman, R. L., 1, 17, 20, 21, 78, 85–102
Shantz, C. U., 1, 3–21, 71, 83
Shantz, D. W., 1, 3–21
Shure, M. B., 4, 5, 8, 21
Shweder, R. A., 5, 20, 56, 58, 59, 69
Silverman, I. W., 73, 83
Sinclair, H., 53
Smetana, J. G., 58, 59, 64, 68, 70, 76, 83
Social cognition: analysis of conflict's role in, 3–21; assesments of, 6–9; conclusions on, 18–20; and conflict issues, 9–12, 15–18; developmental levels of, 7, 19–20; discussion of, 15–20; findings on, 9–14; gender differences in, 12, 16, 17, 18, 19; method of studying, 5–9; and pair therapy, 93–96; and sociometric correlates, 9, 13–14, 18
Social impact, and conflict, 9, 13
Social origins of logic. *See* Logic, social origins of
Social preference, and conflict, 9, 13
Sociocognitive conflict: analysis of, 41–54; background on, 41–42; cognitive factors in, 44–47; and cognitive prerequisites, 45; concept of, 42; conclusions on, 52–53; experimental results on, 42–44; gender differences in, 48, 51; imitation or confrontation in, 44–45; and partner's cognitive level, 46; resolution of, necessary, 46–47; and restructuring, 43–44; social factors in, 47–52; and testing situation, 48–52
Sociometric status: findings on, 13–41, 18; measures of, 9
Speicher-Dubin, B., 74, 76, 83
Spivack, G., 4, 5, 8, 21
Stanley, S., 76, 83
Stone, A., 23*n*
Stone, C., 92, 101

Stone, C. A., 25, 30, 37, 39
Sugarman, S., 23*n*
Sullivan, H. S., 88, 90–91, 102
Sxeminska, A., 54

T

Taranto, M. A., 74, 83
Templin, T., 3*n*
Test of Logical Thinking (TOLT), 77
Testing situation: child's perception of, 49–51; role expectations in, 51–52; as social event, 48–49, 51
Tisak, M., 56, 70
Tisher, R. P., 30, 39
Tobin, K. G., 77, 83
Turiel, E., 5, 8, 21, 56, 58, 59, 66, 67, 68–69, 70, 72, 83

V

Valiant, G. L., 27, 38
Volpe, J., 17, 21
Vygotsky, L. S., 23, 25–26, 29, 34, 36, 39

W

Walton, M. D., 56, 60, 70
Watson, J. D., 34, 39
Wattanawaha, N., 30, 38
Werner, H., 86, 102
Wertsch, J. V., 25, 30, 34, 37, 39
Wonderly, D., 72, 82

Y

Youniss, J., 17, 21

Z

Zone of proximal development, 25